SMART SKETCH BOOK 2

Oogie Art's step-by-step guide to drawing still life objects in charcoal.

Oogie Art

Oogie Art's SmartSketchbook™
An Expert's Guide to Still Life in Charcoal
First Edition, Copyright © 2015

Produced and Edited by
Oogie Art
New York, NY

© Text
Oogie Art

© Photographs
Licensed under Oogie Art®

Directed by
Wook Choi

Assistant Directed by
Clara Lu

Drawings by
Jee Hwang

Tips by
Wook Choi

Published and Distributed by
Oogie Publishing House
New York, NY
www.oogiepublishinghouse.com
(212) 714-1011

ISBN 978-0-9855809-3-3
Printed in the United States

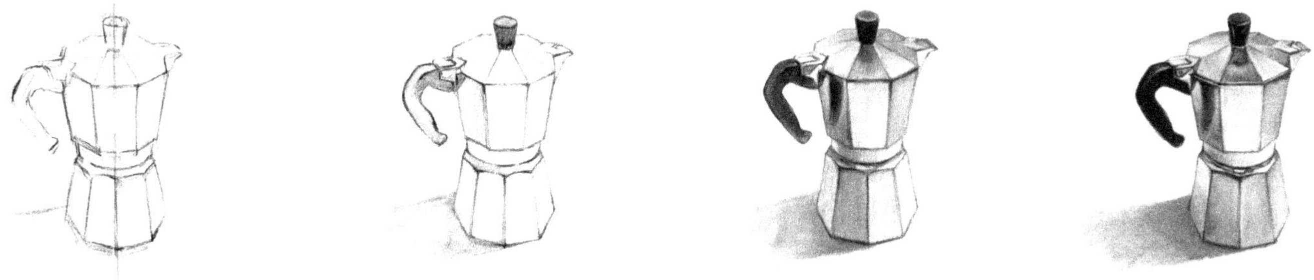

CONTENTS

Introduction to Charcoal

Dry drawing tools are easier to express the intention of the artist in comparison to aqueous tools since the intensity and density of the line are controlled directly by pressure. Charcoal is one of the most common soft dry mediums and is easy to smudge. It is ideal for quick sketching like gesture drawing.

What you'll need

- Compressed Charcoal of different grades (soft, medium and hard)
- Vine charcoal
- 1 Vinyl eraser
- 1 Kneaded eraser
- 1 Can of fixative spray

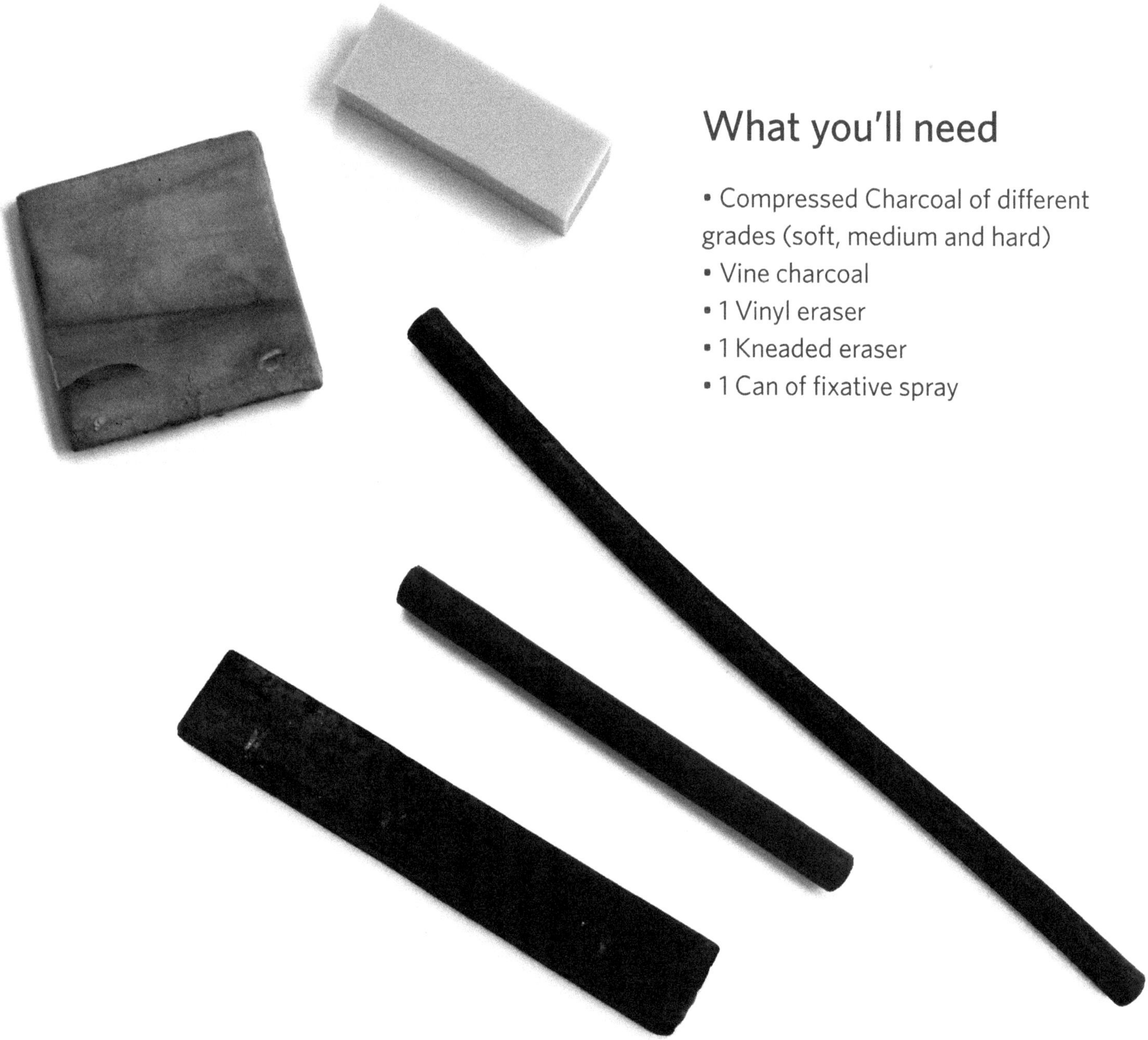

Forms and Types of Charcoal

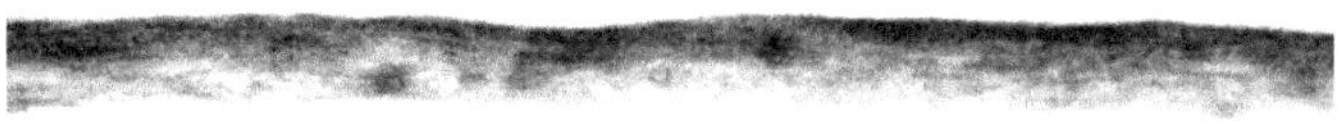

Vine Charcoal

Most commonly used to start a drawing, best for creating a wide range of values, easiest to smudge

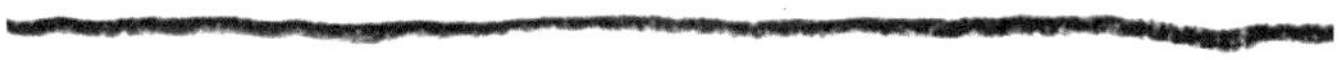

Aqueous (water) based Compressed Charcoal

- Round shape: for general mark making
- Square shape or broken pieces: for creating sharp edges, rough textures, or fine thin lines

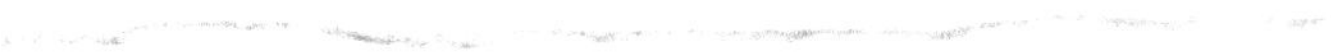

Charcoal Pencil

Fine detail work

Oil Based Charcoal Sticks

Compressed Charcoal

Typically used to make darker marks by layers of smudging and is harder to erase

*Some manufacturers make white or brown compressed charcoal.

Charcoal Techniques

Mastering the versatility of charcoal is important in rendering different textures and creating highlights and shadows. Try creating the following textures yourself using vine and compressed charcoal. Remember to have fun and experiment.

Smudging: For creating a range of value over an area

- Use a cloth or your thumb to cover a larger area
- Use a finger for both general and detailed work

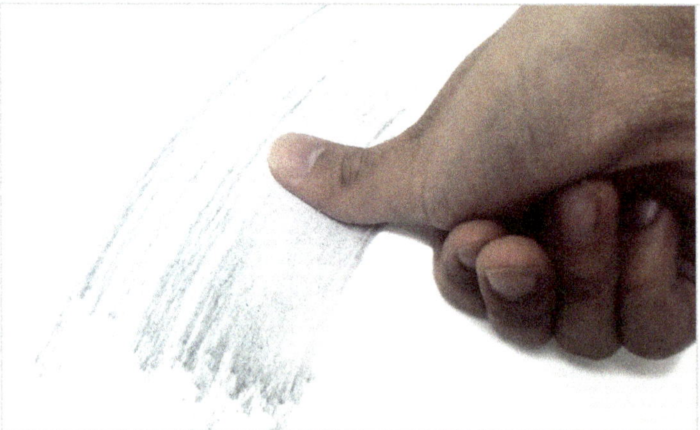

Eraser: For adding highlights covered up by smudging

- Use to create sharp areas of highlight
- Use to clean your line work
- Create highlights on your objects

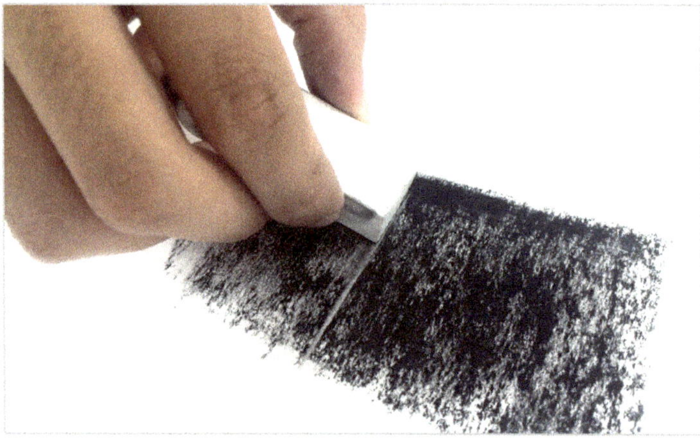

Practice the tutorials on the next page to improve your charcoal drawing ability.

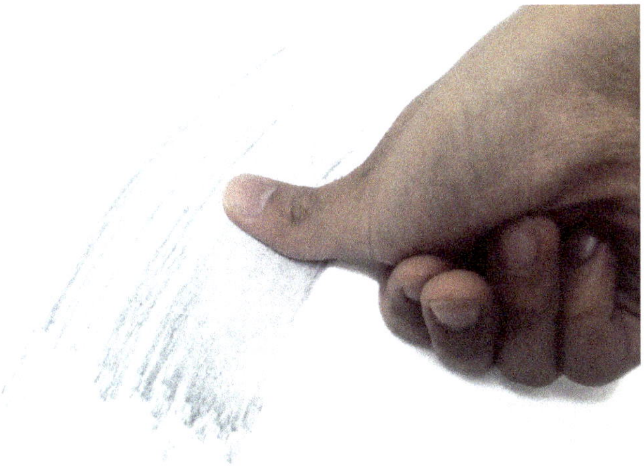

1. Smudge a large area to create the first layer of shading and press harder to apply the vine charcoal on the paper.

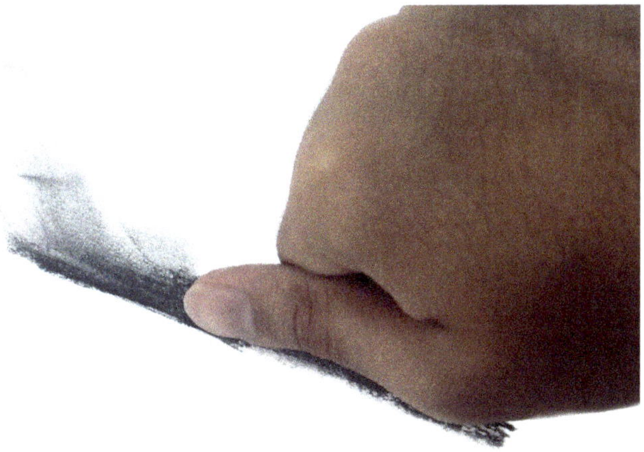

2. Use the edge of your finger to define the sharp edges of an object.

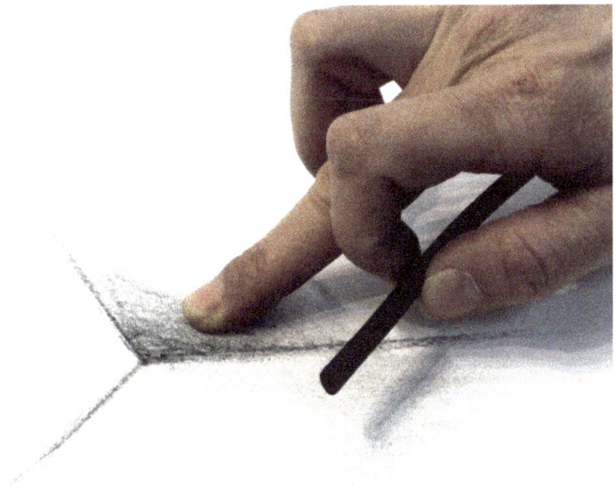

3. Create a second layer of shading in vine and repeat 2-3 times.

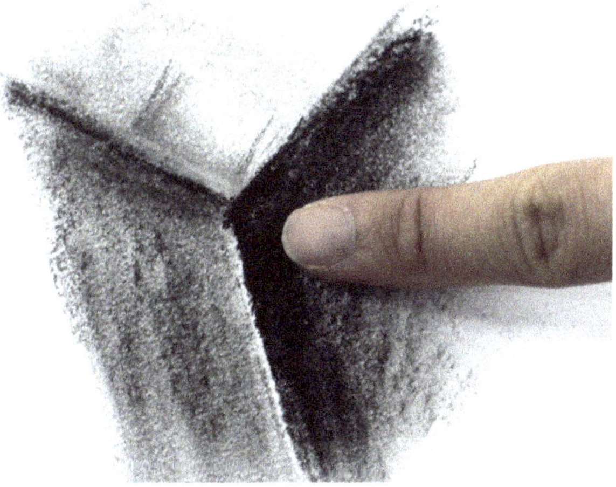

4. Use compressed charcoal to darken your shading and smudge accordingly.

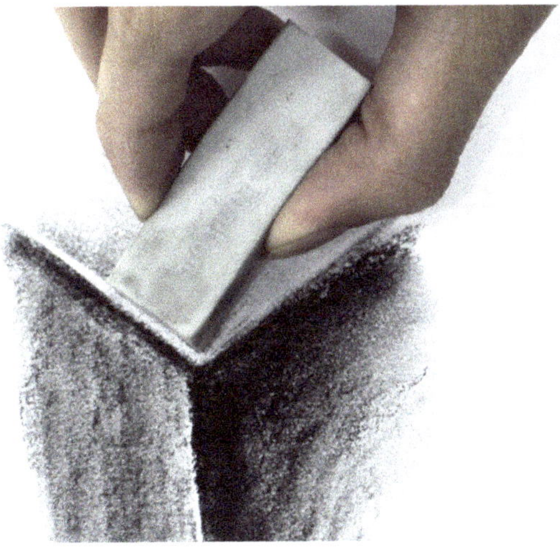

5. Use the sharp part of a vinyl eraser to define objects and to create highlights.

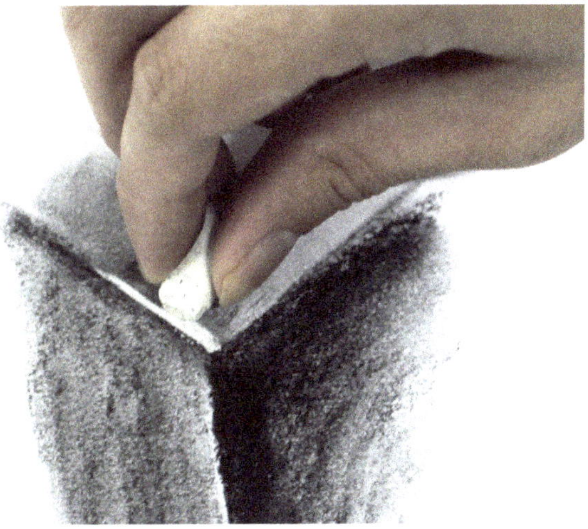

6. Create highlights with white charcoal.

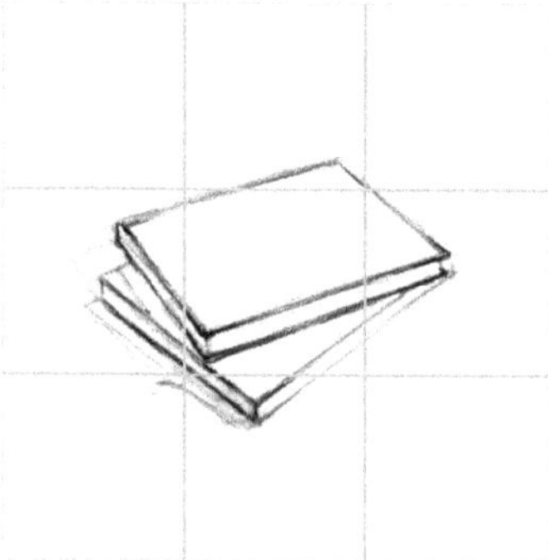

Sketch the general composition of the books using vine charcoal.

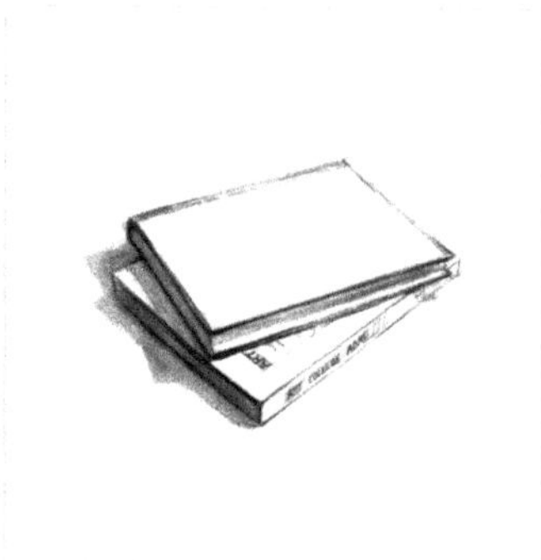

Identify the direction of the light source and shade in the general areas of shadow using vine charcoal.

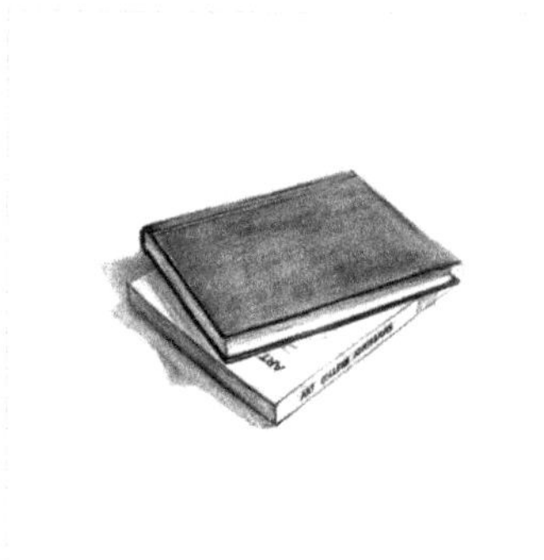

Continue to identify the darks, lights, and middle tones using a combination of vine and compressed charcoal.

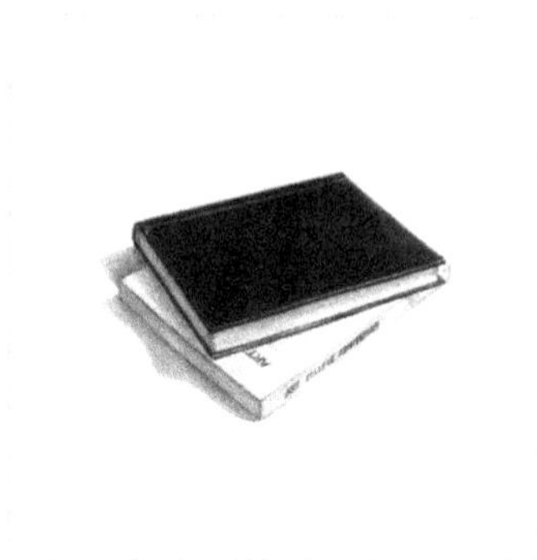

Make sure your book drawing is fully developed and the two books are defined. Draw the details such as the letters in the title and page texture in charcoal pencil or with a sharp edge of a broken piece of charcoal. Then create highlights with an eraser.

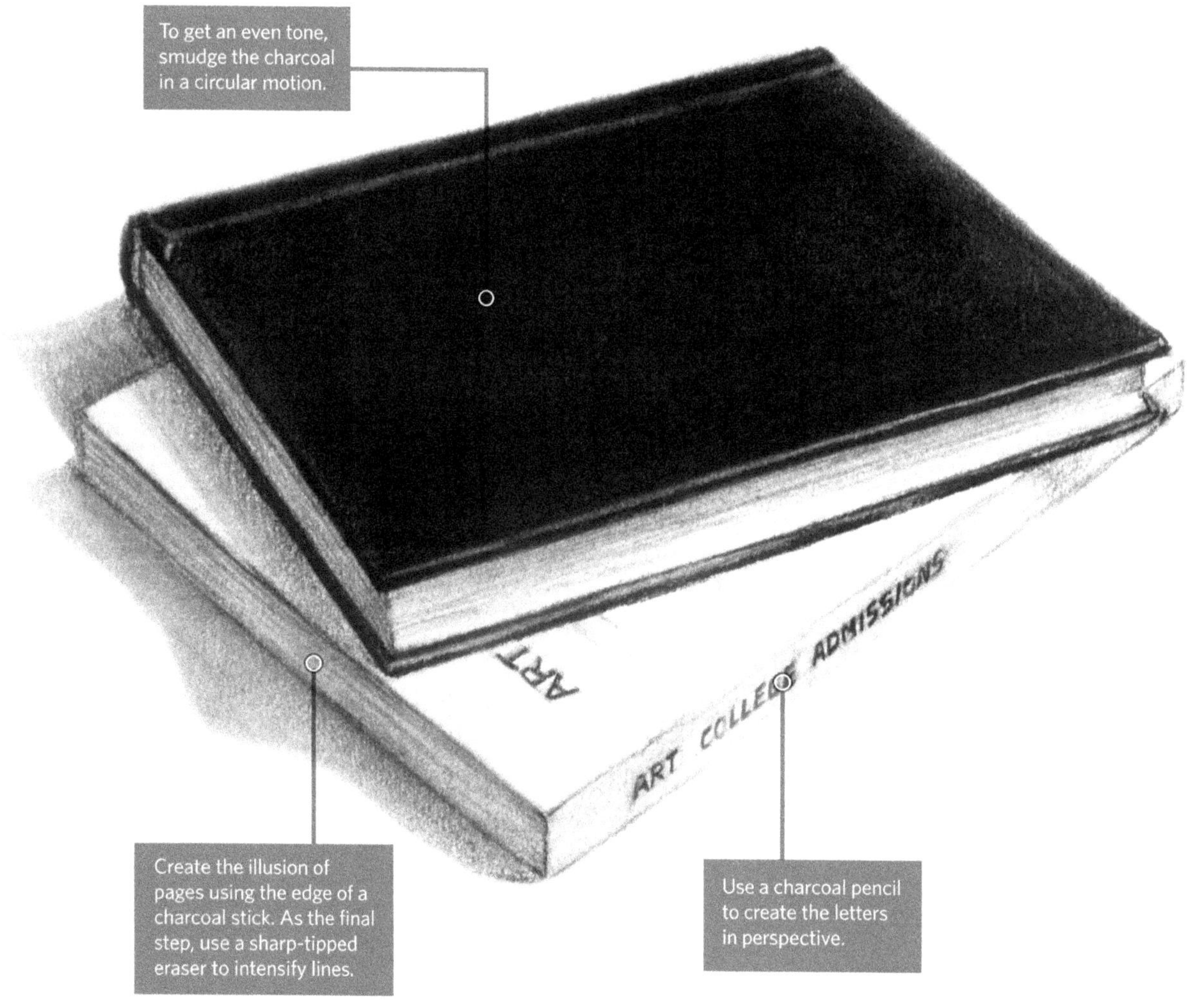

Now try drawing the book yourself.

Similar to the edges of the cube in the first exercise, keep the respective edges of the books parallel to one another. Keeping these edges parallel is key to rendering these objects in correct proportion and perspective to one another. Make sure you reserve the details for the very last, smudge them lightly, and then leave them alone.

Now try drawing the books using the reference picture without any grid lines.

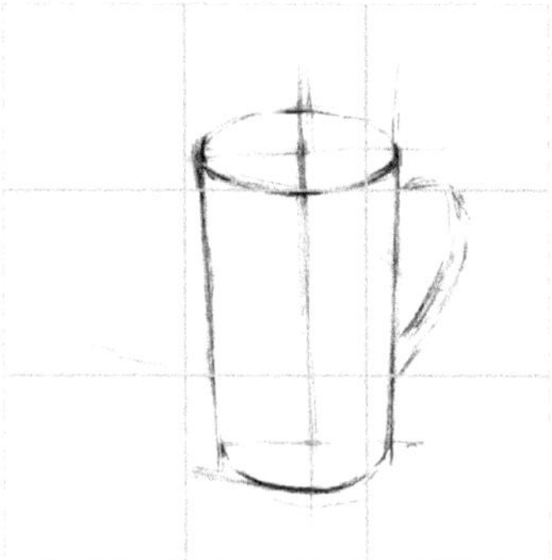

Sketch the general shape of the cup in vine charcoal. It's like combining a cylinder with a handle.

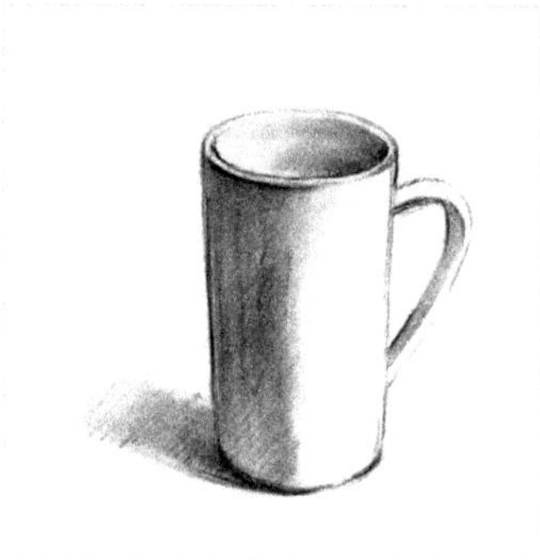

Identify the light source and shade in the general area of shadow in vine charcoal.

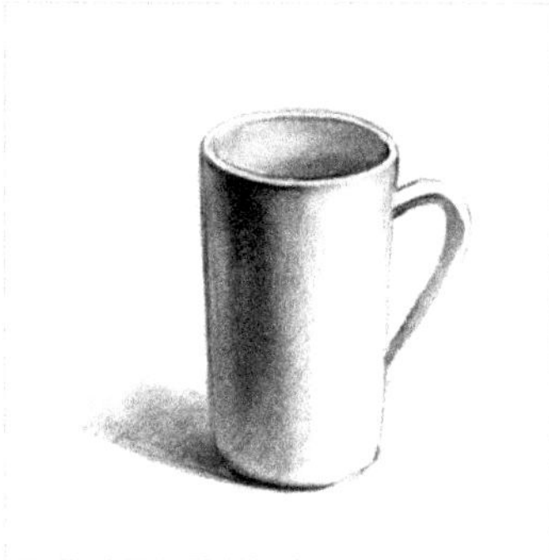

Continue to create full range of value with compressed charcoal.

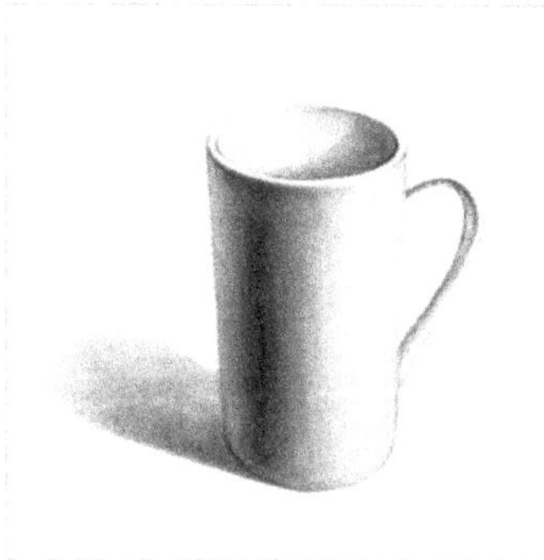

Make sure to make the dark parts darker with compressed charcoal, add reflected light and highlight with an eraser.

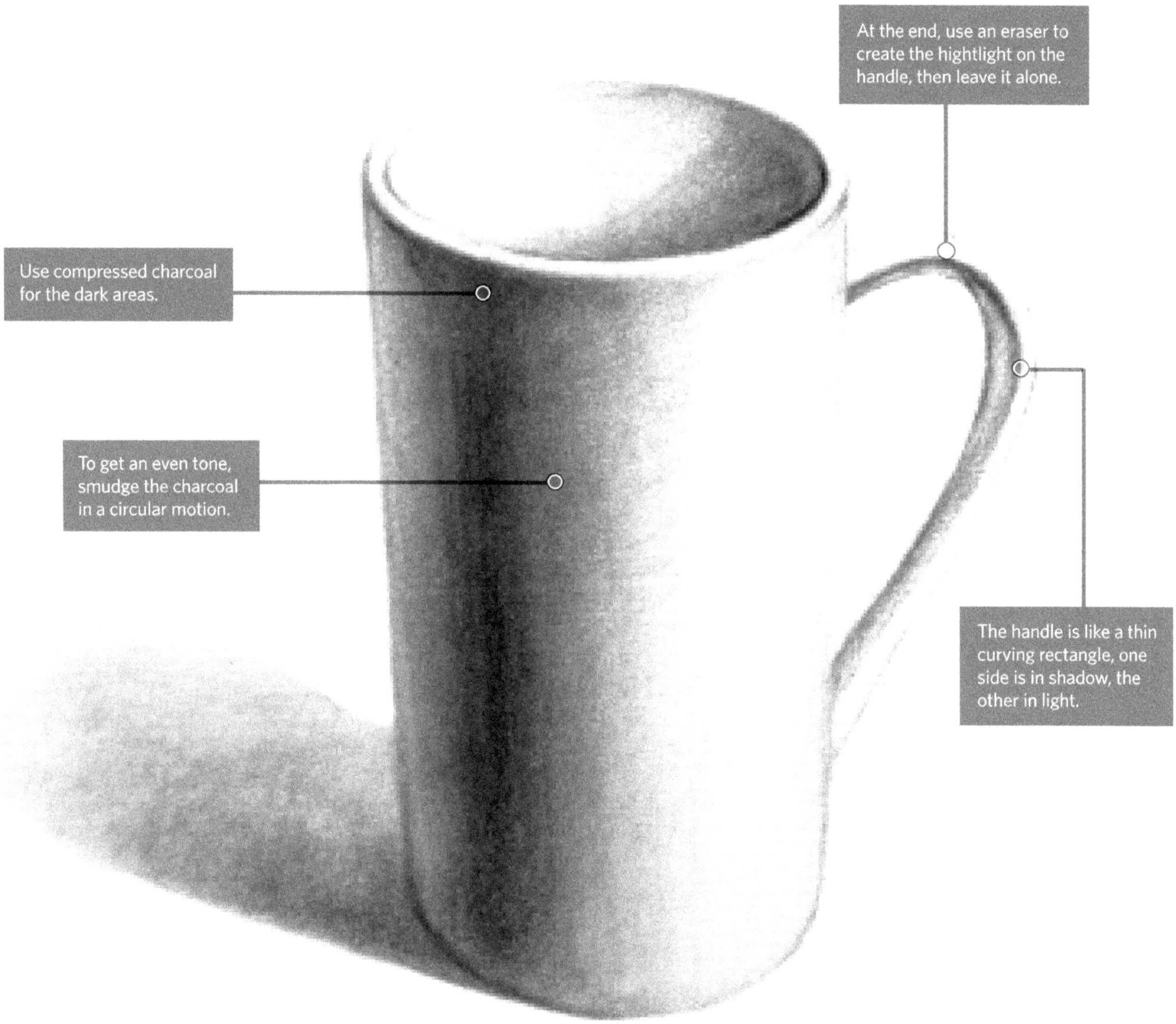

Now try drawing the cup yourself.

Shade in general areas using vine charcoal and smudging in a circular motion to get an even tone. Then use compressed charcoal to darken specific areas of shadow. The most important thing to remember when drawing any cup is that the shadows casted on the outside of the cup fall on the opposite side inside of the cup.

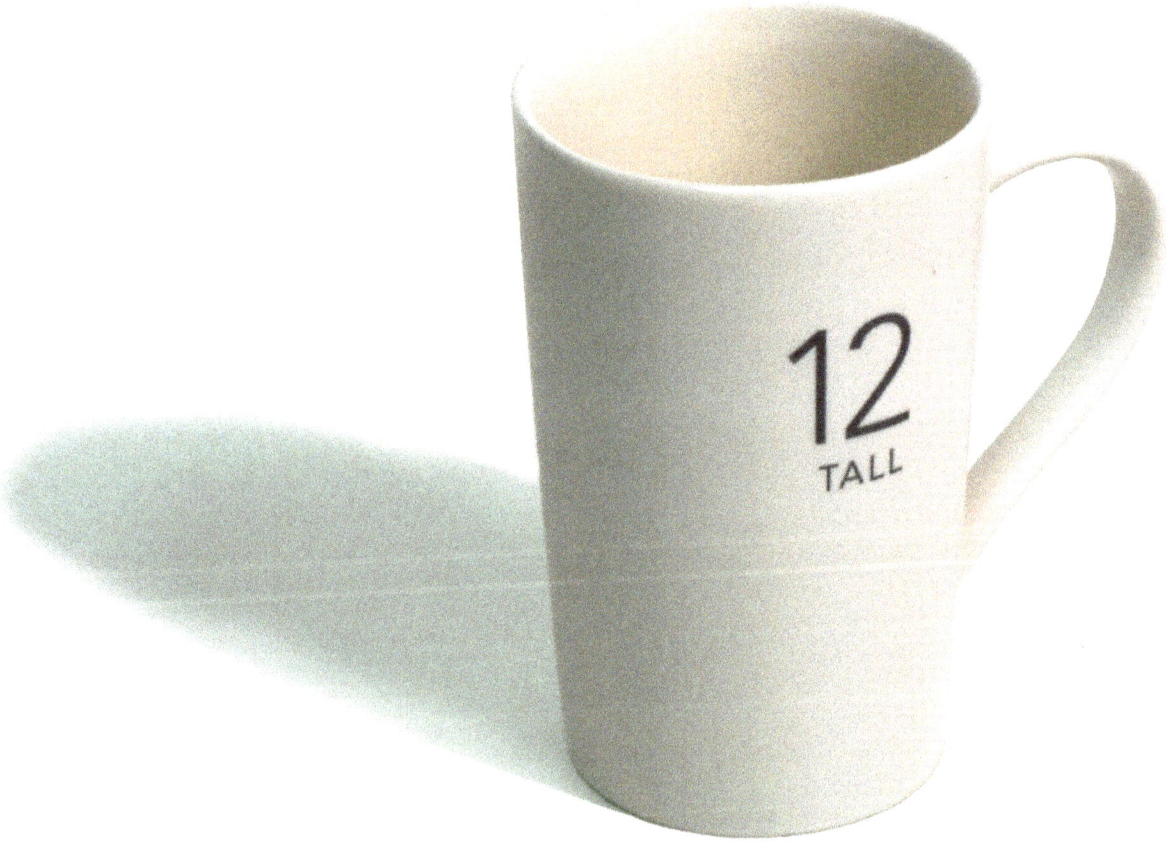

Now try drawing the cup using the reference picture without any grid lines.

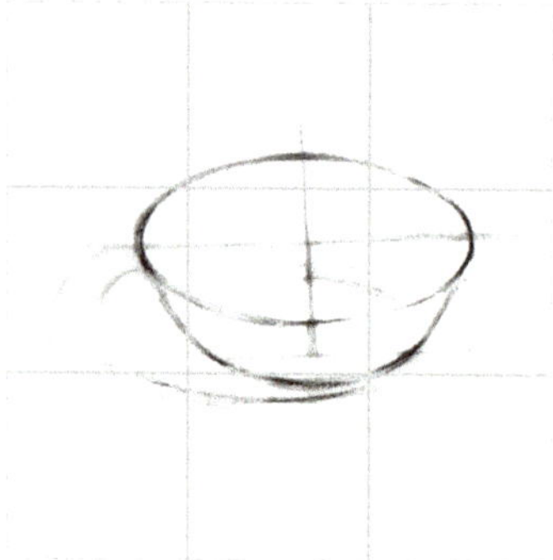

Sketch out the general shape of the bowl using vine charcoal. Use lines to help you in drawing the bowl's lip, remember, it's an ellipse.

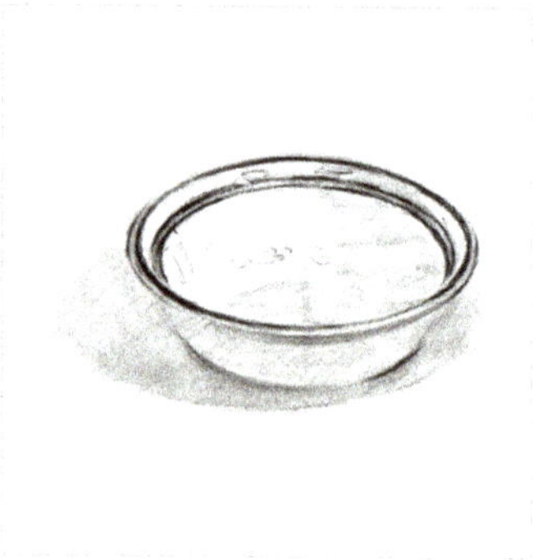

Begin to add in the general areas of shadow with vine charcoal.

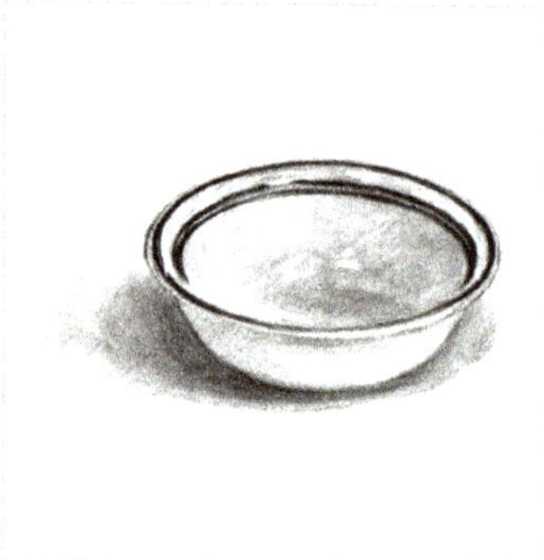

Continue to develop the darks, lights, and middle tones using a mix of vine and compressed charcoal.

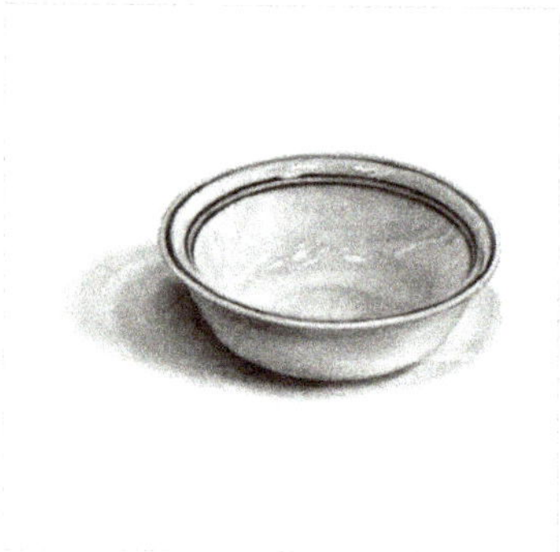

Use the entire range of tones to completely develop your drawing. Draw in the crisp lines and create the hightlights last.

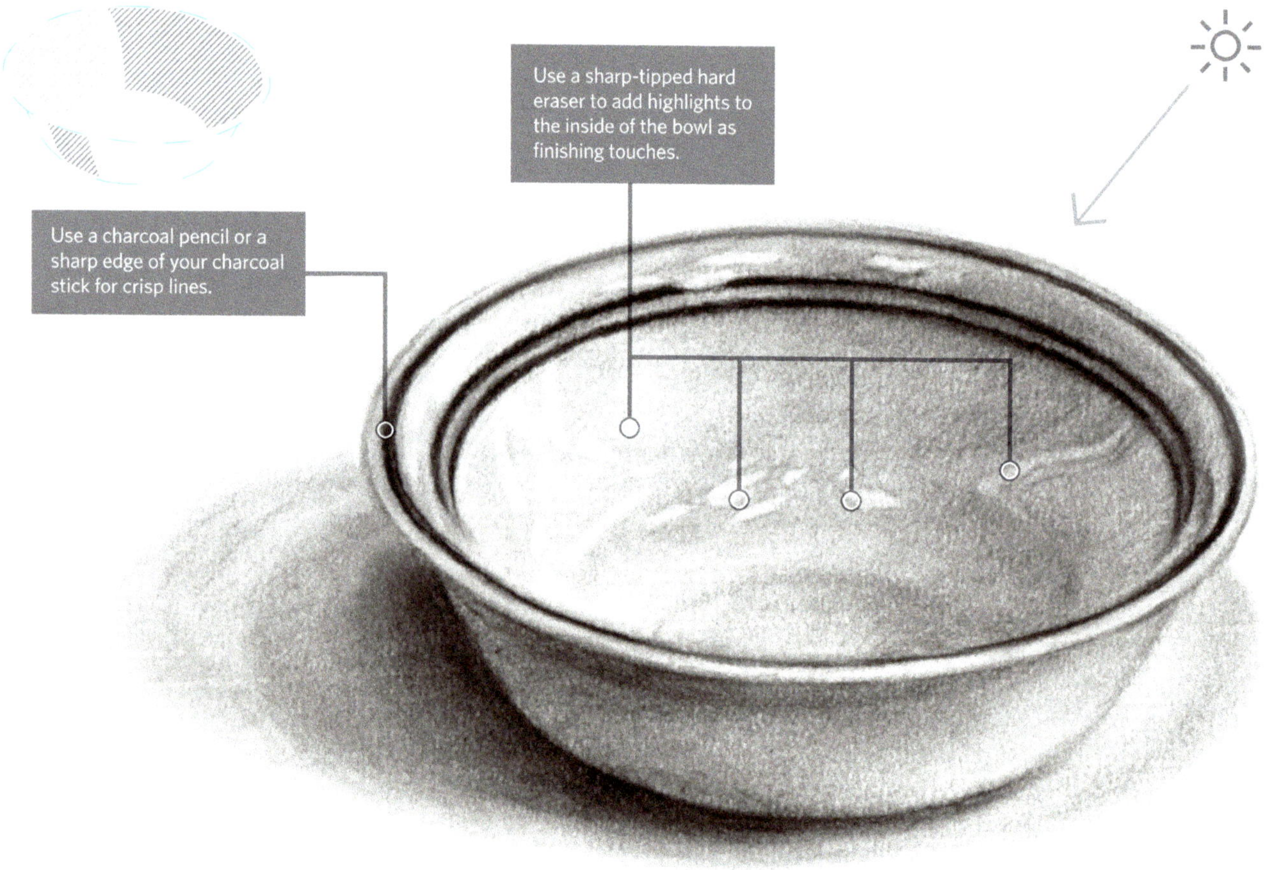

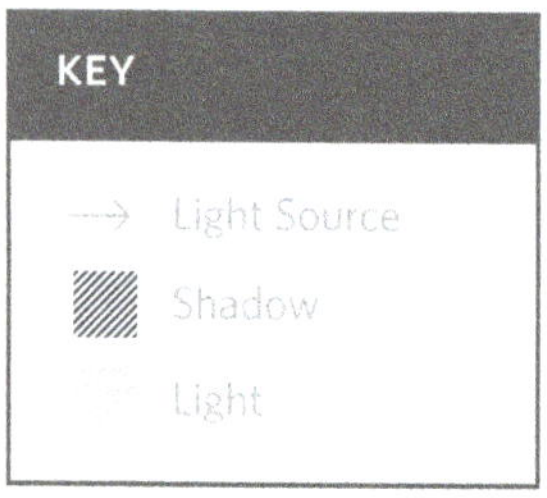

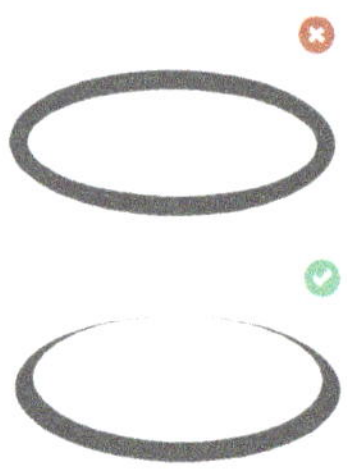

Now try drawing the bowl yourself.

Drawing a bowl is like drawing a cylinder with one end rounded in. Don't be intimidated by its shiny surface. Instead focus on the general areas of shadow before going into the details. Work with vine charcoal first to put in the general areas of shadow. Then use compressed charcoal to create darker areas of shadow. To finalize your drawing, use a charcoal pencil or the sharp edge of a charcoal stick to create crisp lines. The very last step is to create highlights using the edge of a hard eraser rather than a soft eraser. Then leave your drawing alone.

When drawing reflective surfaces, it's important to use the sharp edge of an eraser to create light reflections to create the illusion of a shiny surface.

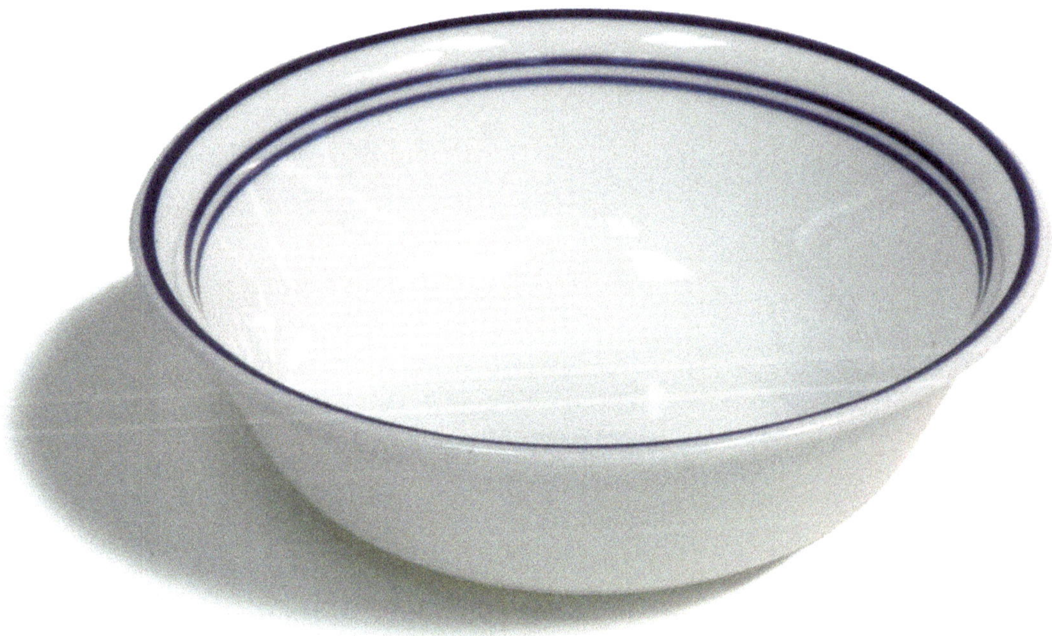

Now try drawing the bowl using the reference picture without any grid lines.

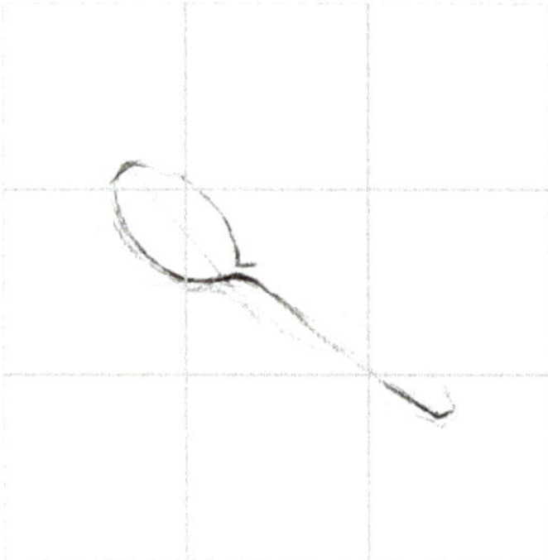

Use vine charcoal to sketch the general shape of the spoon. Create a center line to help you with symmetry.

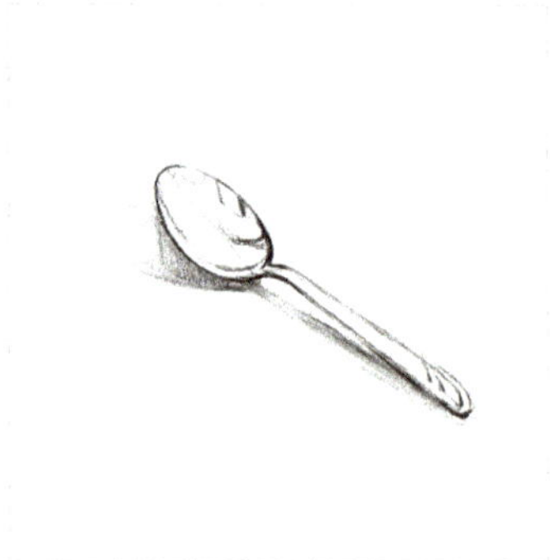

Identify the direction of the light source and shade in the general areas of shadow using vine charcoal.

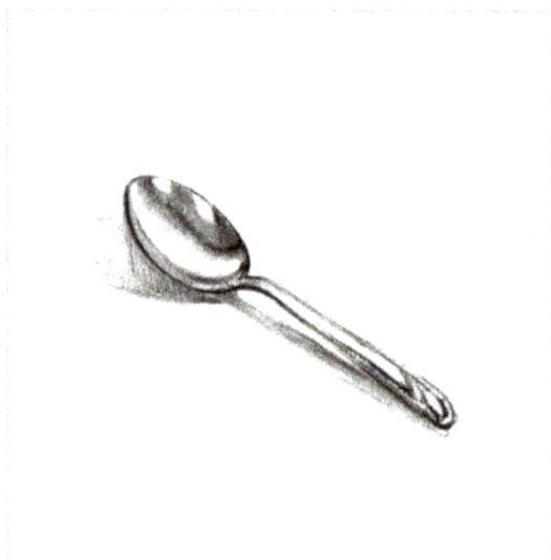

Continue to identify the darks, lights, and middle tones using a combination of vine and compressed charcoal.

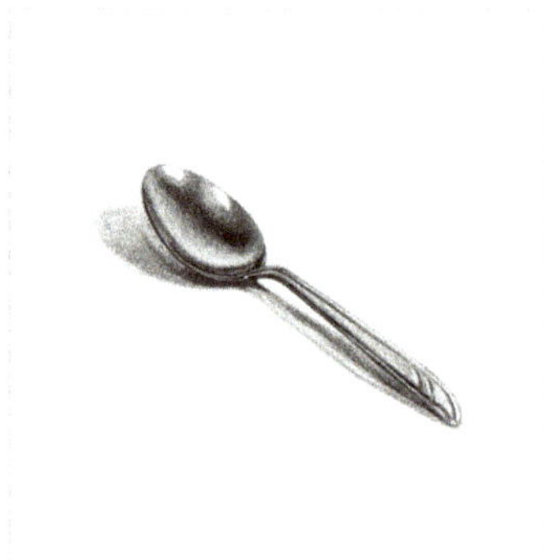

Make sure your spoon drawing is fully developed. Use a charcoal pencil or sharp edge of a broken charcoal stick to draw details like the reflections in the spoon. Then create highlights with an eraser.

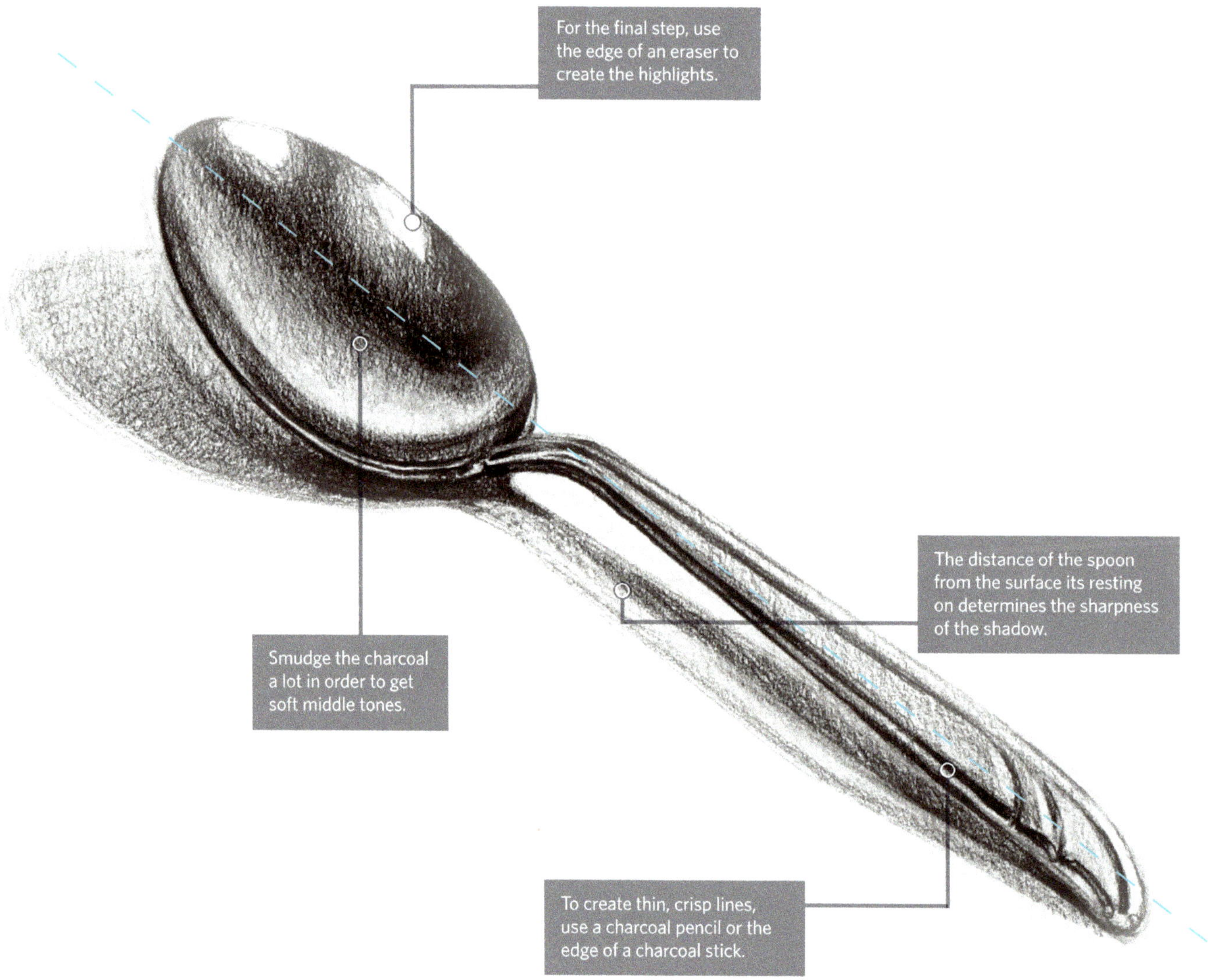

Now try drawing the spoon yourself.

Spoons can be challenging objects to draw because of their varying thicknesses, individual engravings, and also their metallic and curved reflections. Keep in mind to work gradually from general to specific in order to maintain the illusion of a curved spoon, otherwise your spoon may appear oddly bent. Remember to define the highlights and the sharp edges at the very end. The more details you can capture, the more realistic the spoon your rendering in charcoal will become.

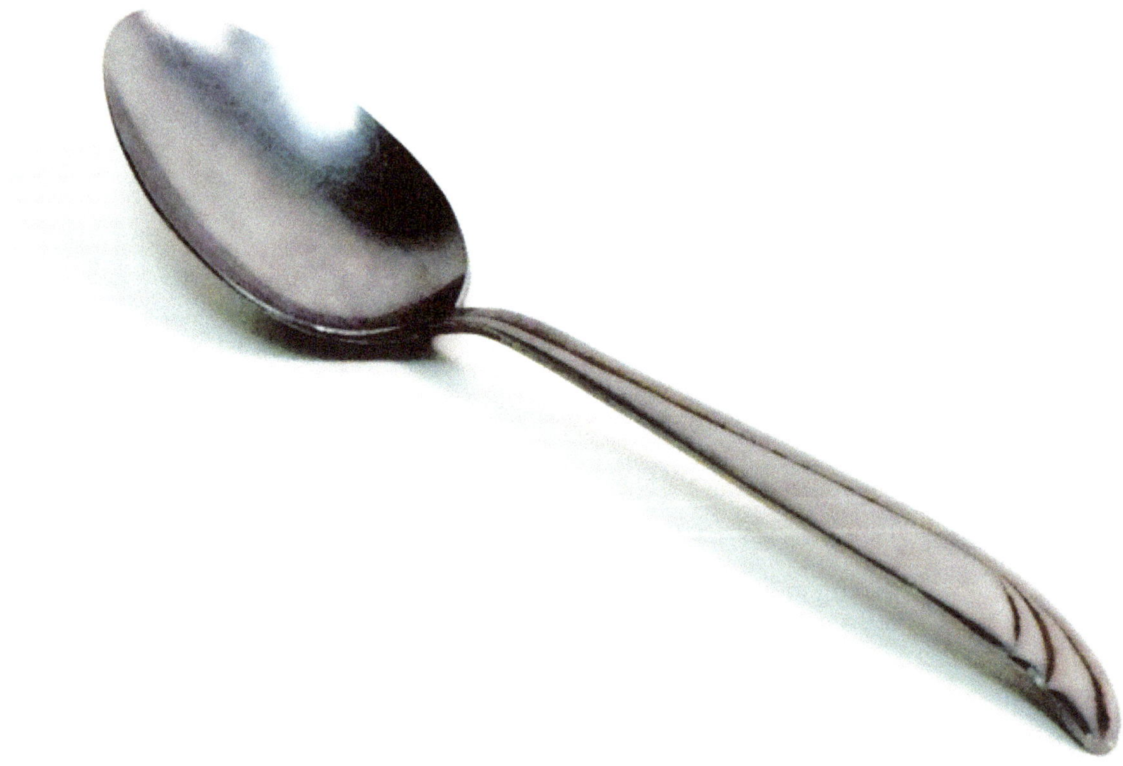

Now try drawing the spoon using the reference picture without any grid lines.

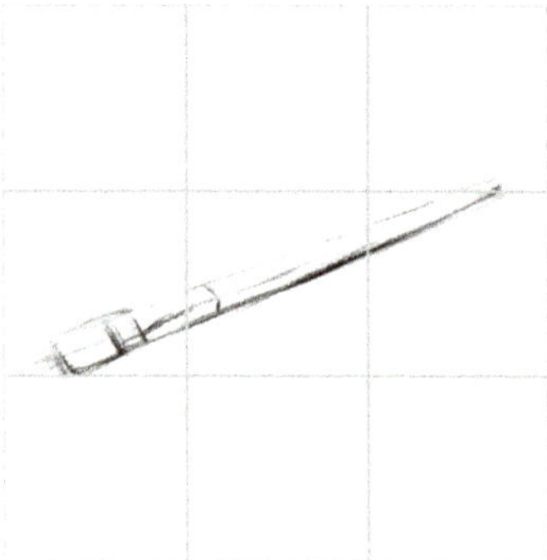

Use vine charcoal to sketch the general shape of the brush. Create a center line to help you determine the shape.

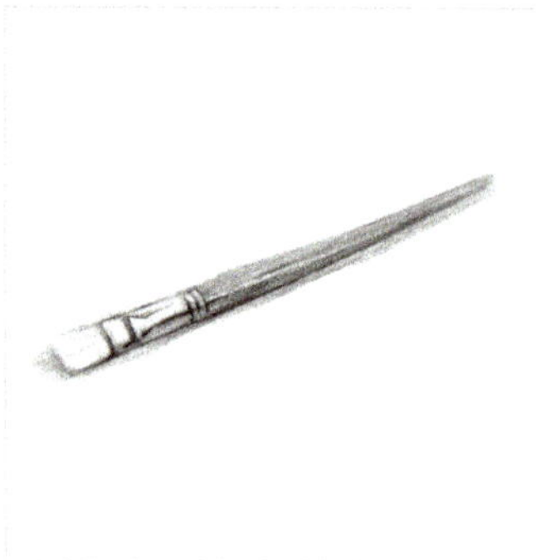

Identify the direction of the light source and use vine charcoal to shade in the general areas of shadow accordingly.

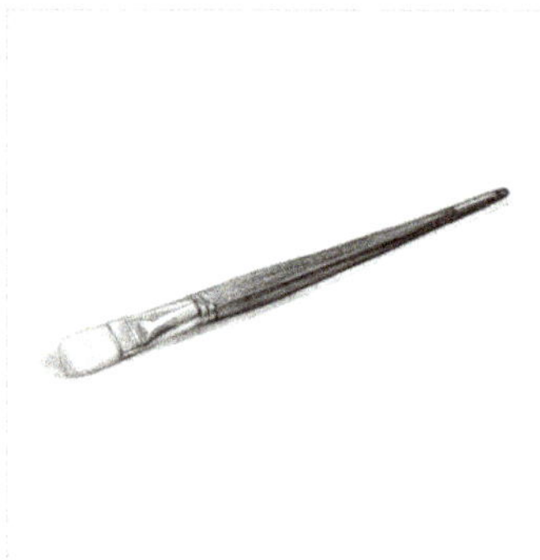

Continue to identify the darks, lights, and middle tones using a combination of vine and compressed charcoal.

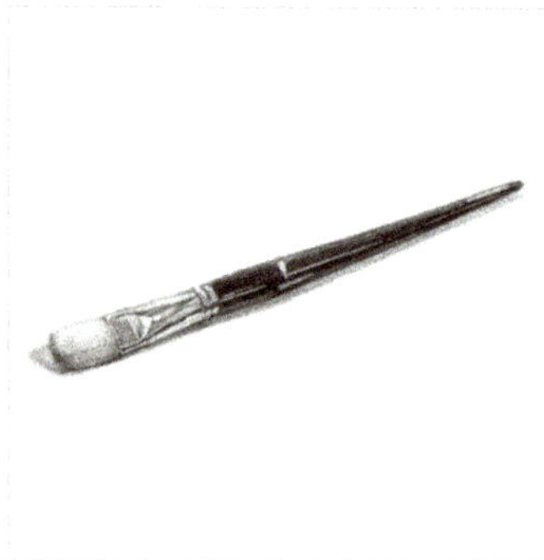

Make sure your brush drawing is fully defined with detail in the metal, hair and wooden handle. Create highlights with an eraser.

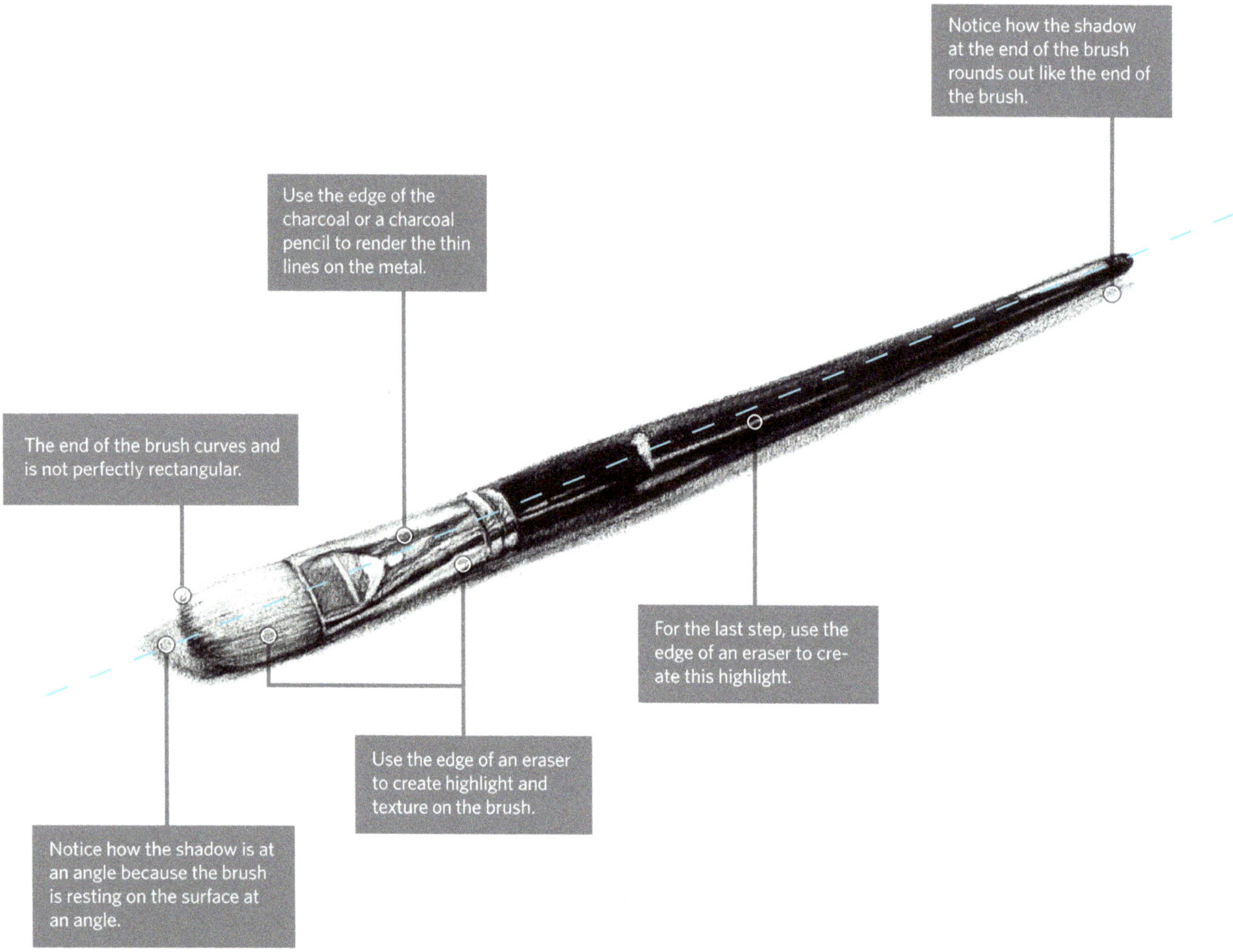

Now try drawing the small brush yourself.

The small brush combines many different techniques and textures, including hair, wood, and metal. Keep in mind how the previous exercises that helped you render volume. Notice where the object changes in shape and texture to create the same illusion when drawing.

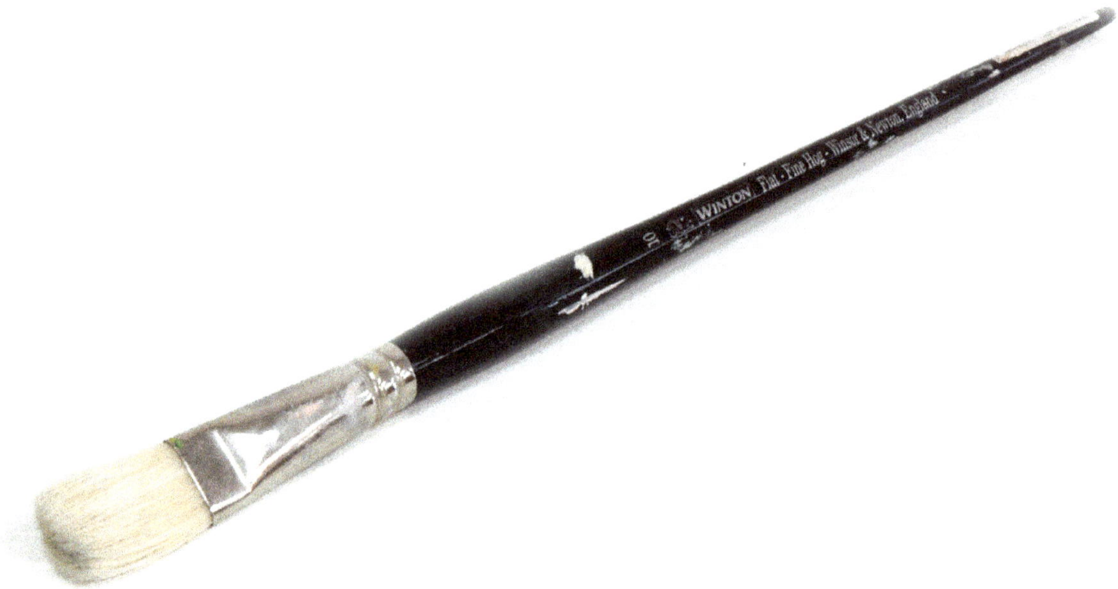

Now try drawing the small brush using the reference picture without any grid lines.

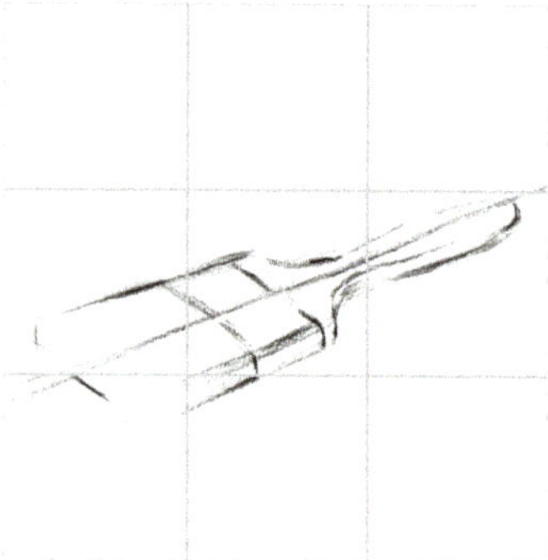

Use vine charcoal to sketch the general shape of the brush, using a center line to help you determine the shape.

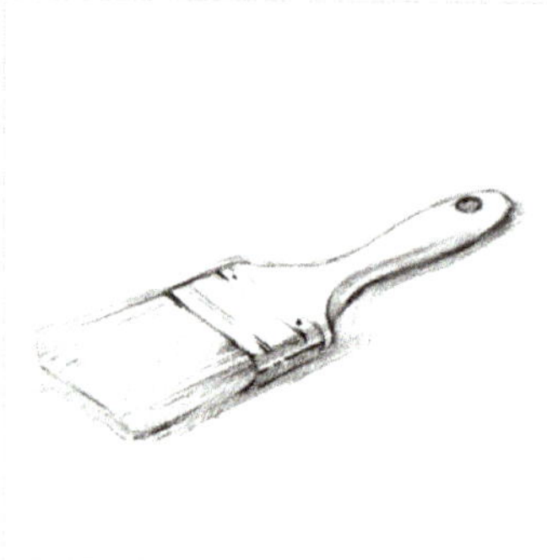

Identify the direction of the light source and shade in the general areas of shadow using vine charcoal.

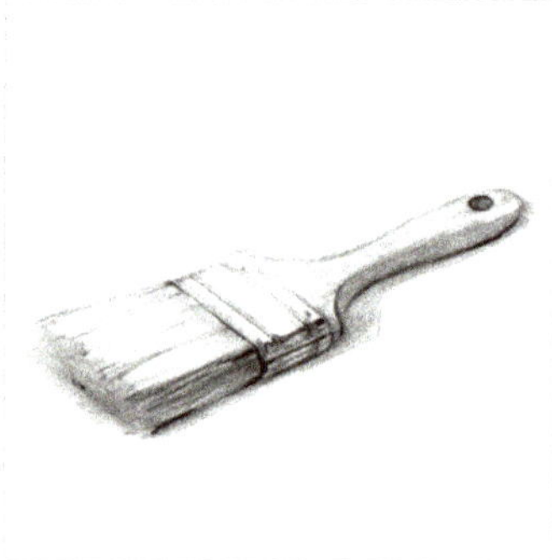

Continue to identify the darks, lights, and middle tones, using mainly vine charcoal.

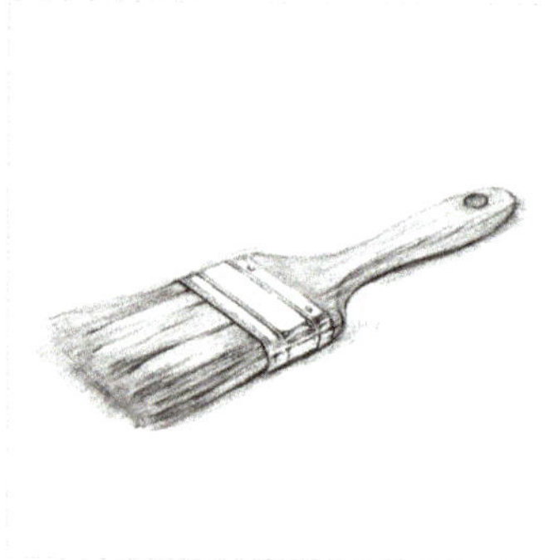

Make sure your brush drawing is fully defined with texture on the metal, hair and wooden handle. Finally, create the highlights with an eraser.

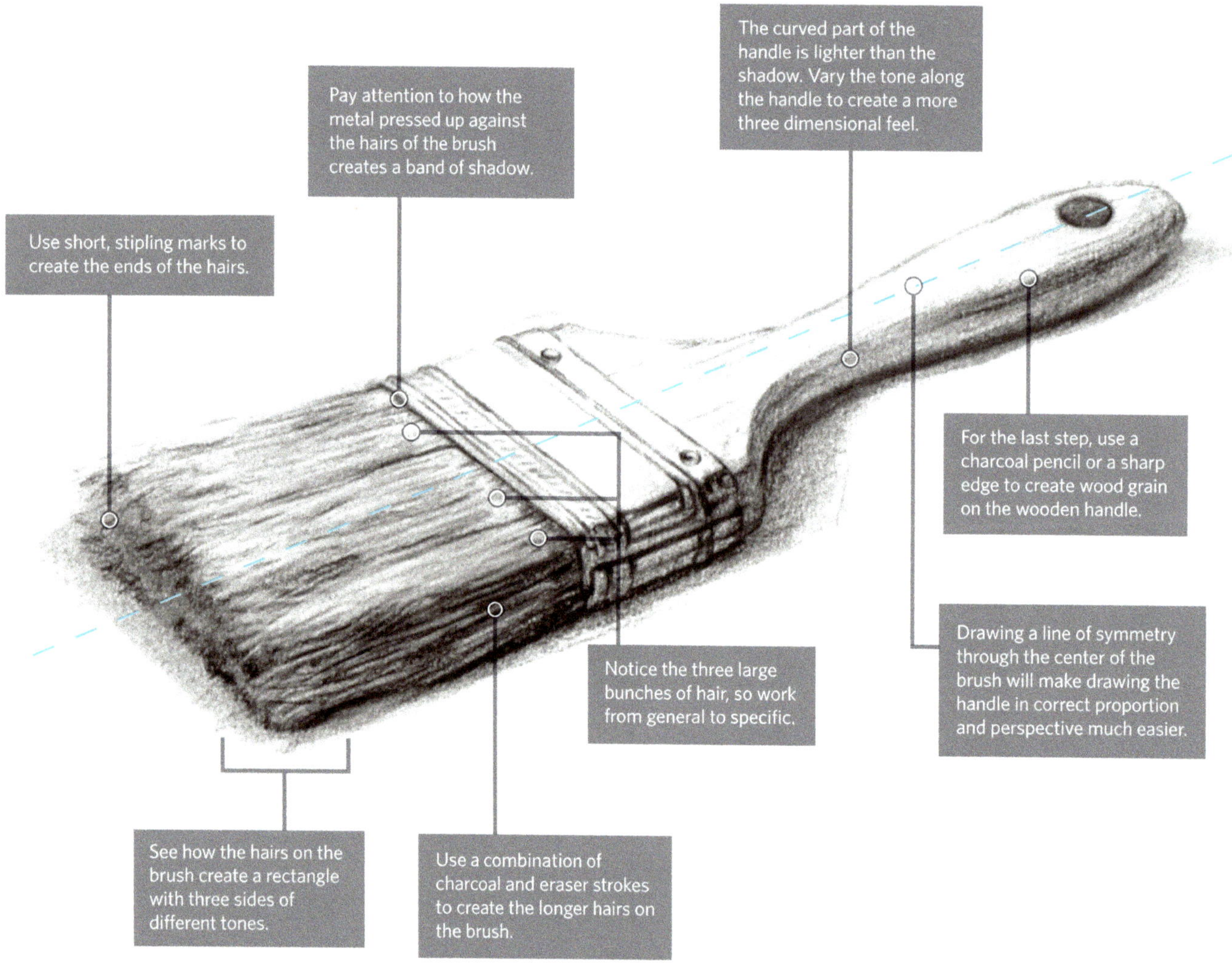

Now try drawing the large brush yourself.

Like the small brush, the large brush is an opportunity for you to practice the techniques you have learned. To further practice rendering hair, metal, and wood grain, remember the different textures and the treatment of charcoal for each: use straight strokes for the hairs, smudge the charcoal for softer areas when rendering metal and wood, and add in details of wood grain and reflection at the very end.

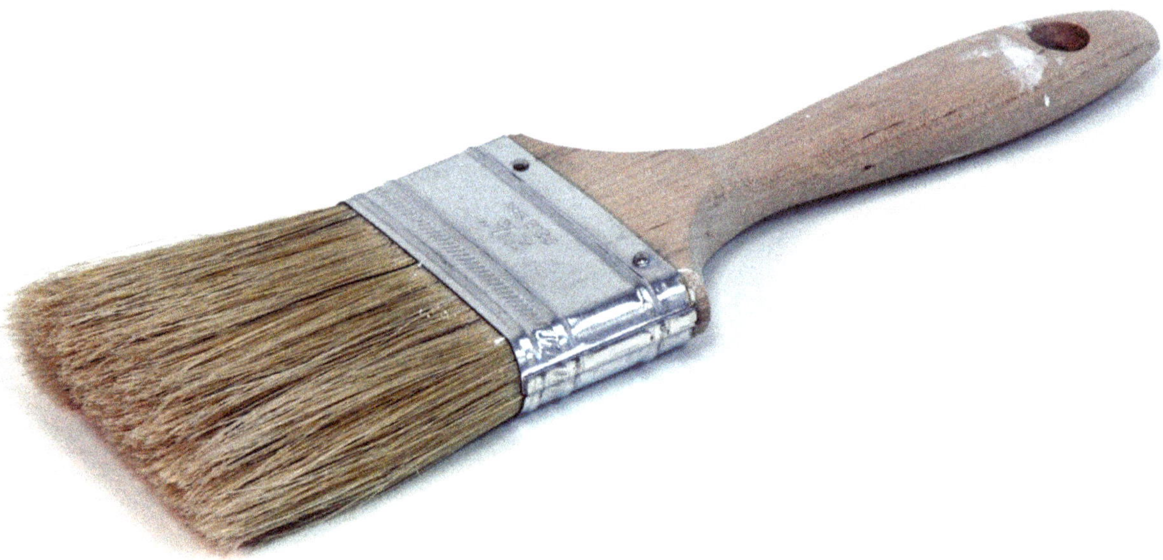

Now try drawing the large brush using the reference picture without any grid lines.

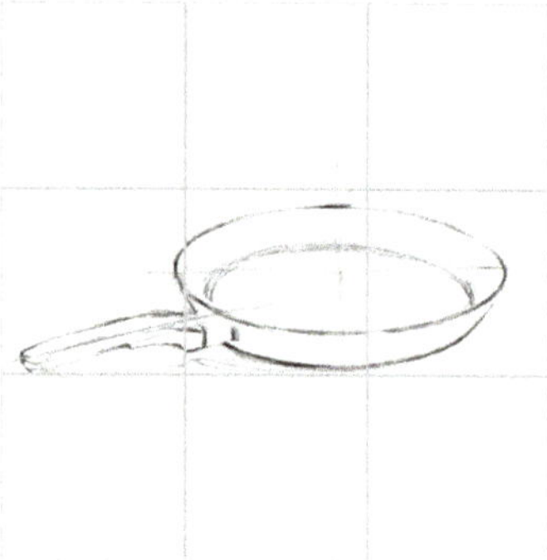

Sketch the general composition of the pan using vine charcoal.

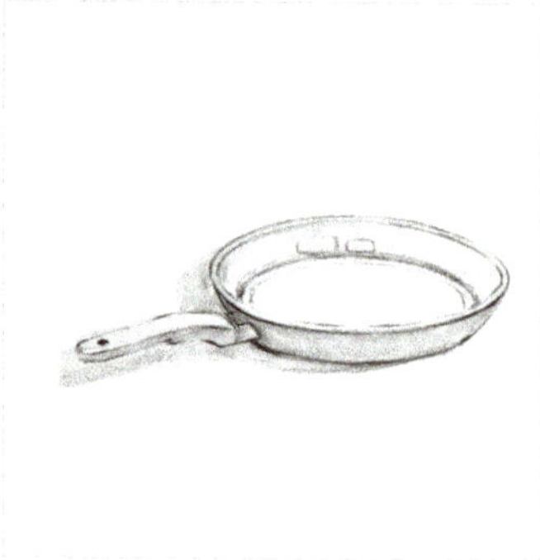

Identify the direction of the light source and shade in the general areas of shadow using vine charcoal.

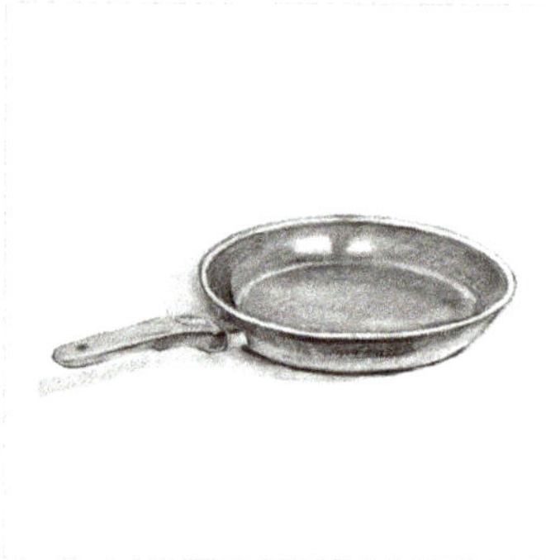

Continue to identify the darks, lights, and middle tones using a conbination of vine and compressed charcoal.

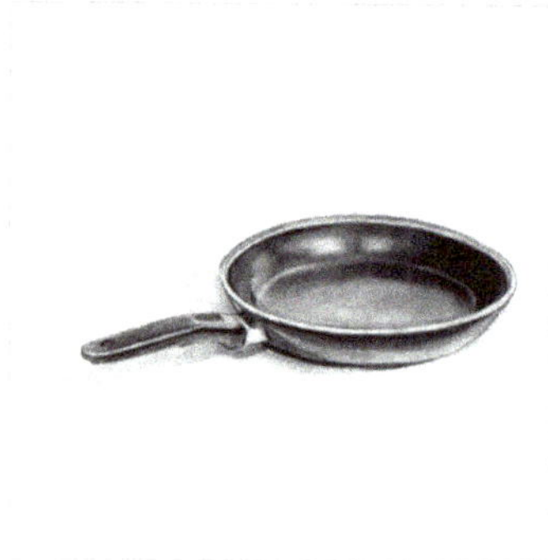

Make sure your frying pan drawing is fully defined with textures. Differentiate between black metal and black plastic handle. Create the highlights with an eraser.

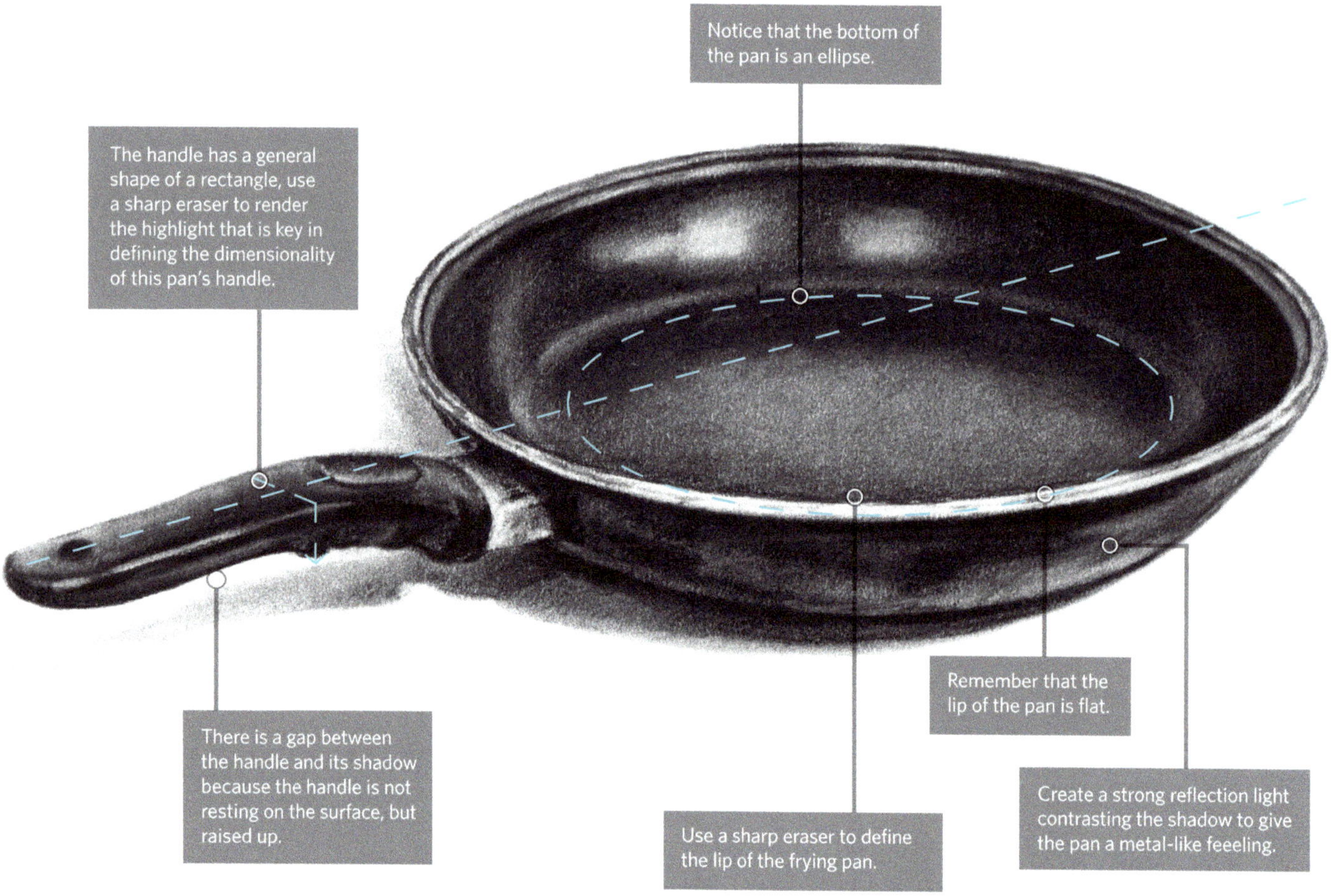

Now try drawing the pan yourself.

The frying pan is more difficult to render than a cup because it is shallower and its handle is longer, which adds more overall perspective to this piece. Pay close attention to the subtleties that define the pan's handle. Look at the reflections on the bottom of the pan and the main lip. Also, like the bowl, the side of shadow and light will be opposite inside the pan versus the outside of the pan. The more details you can capture, the more realistic the pan will appear, but make sure to work from general to detailed.

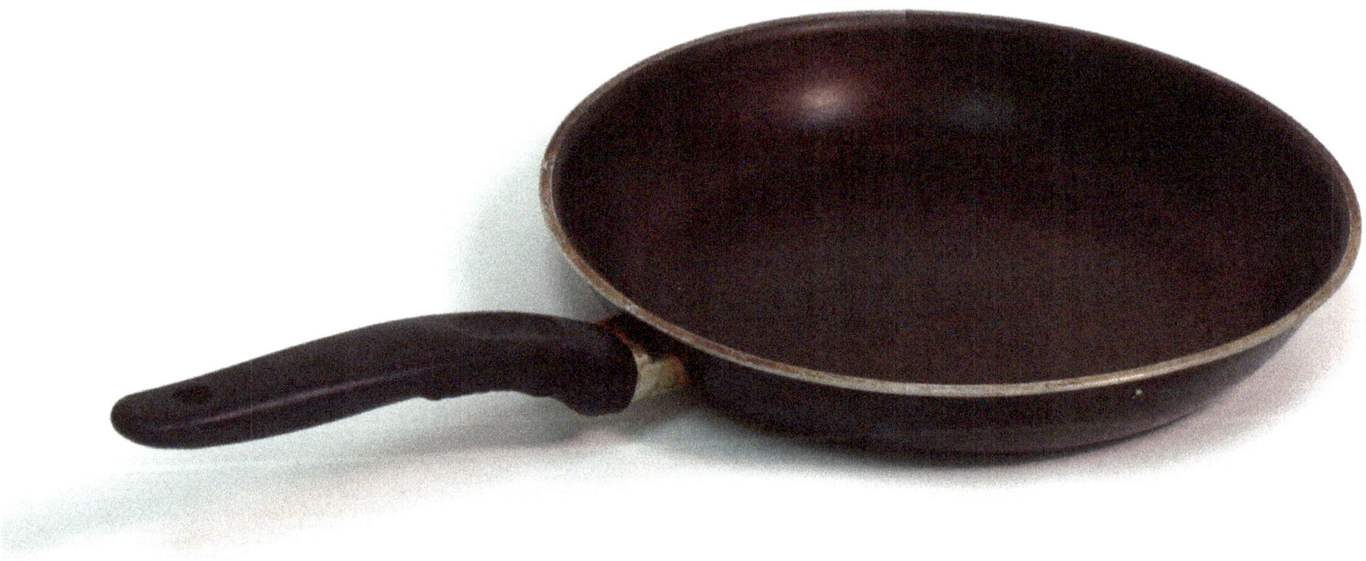

Now try drawing the frying pan using the reference picture without any grid lines.

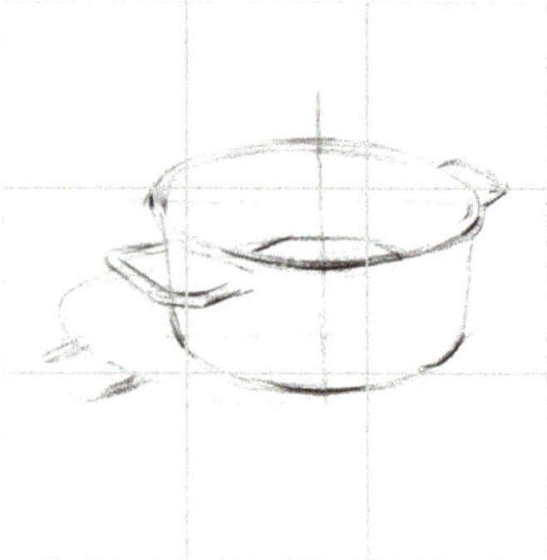

Sketch the general composition of the pot using vine charcoal.

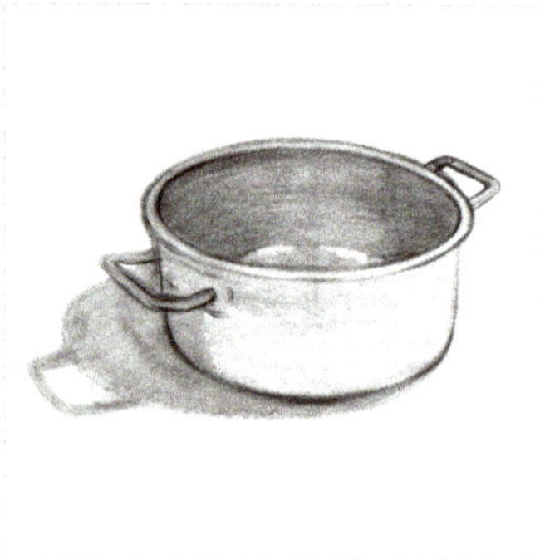

Identify the direction of the light source and shade in the general areas of shadow using vine charcoal.

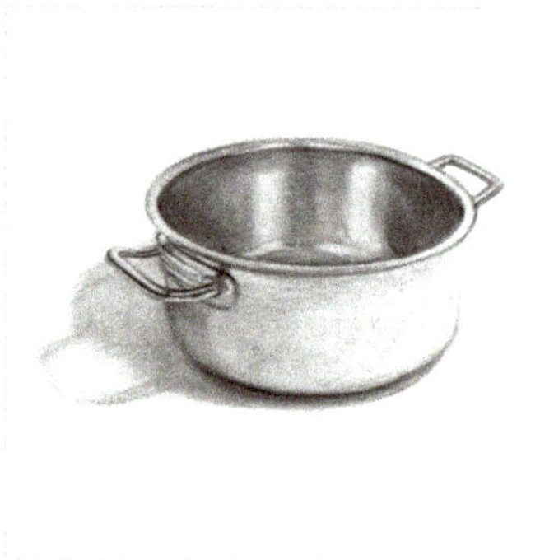

Continue to identify the darks, lights, and middle tones using a combination of vine and compressed charcoal.

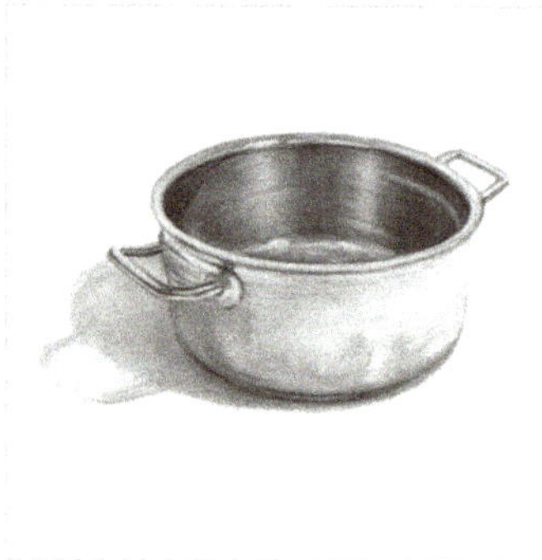

Make sure your metal pot drawing is fully defined. Add varying darkness and texture to the metal and add the highlight with an eraser. Finally, confirm that the handles are parallel.

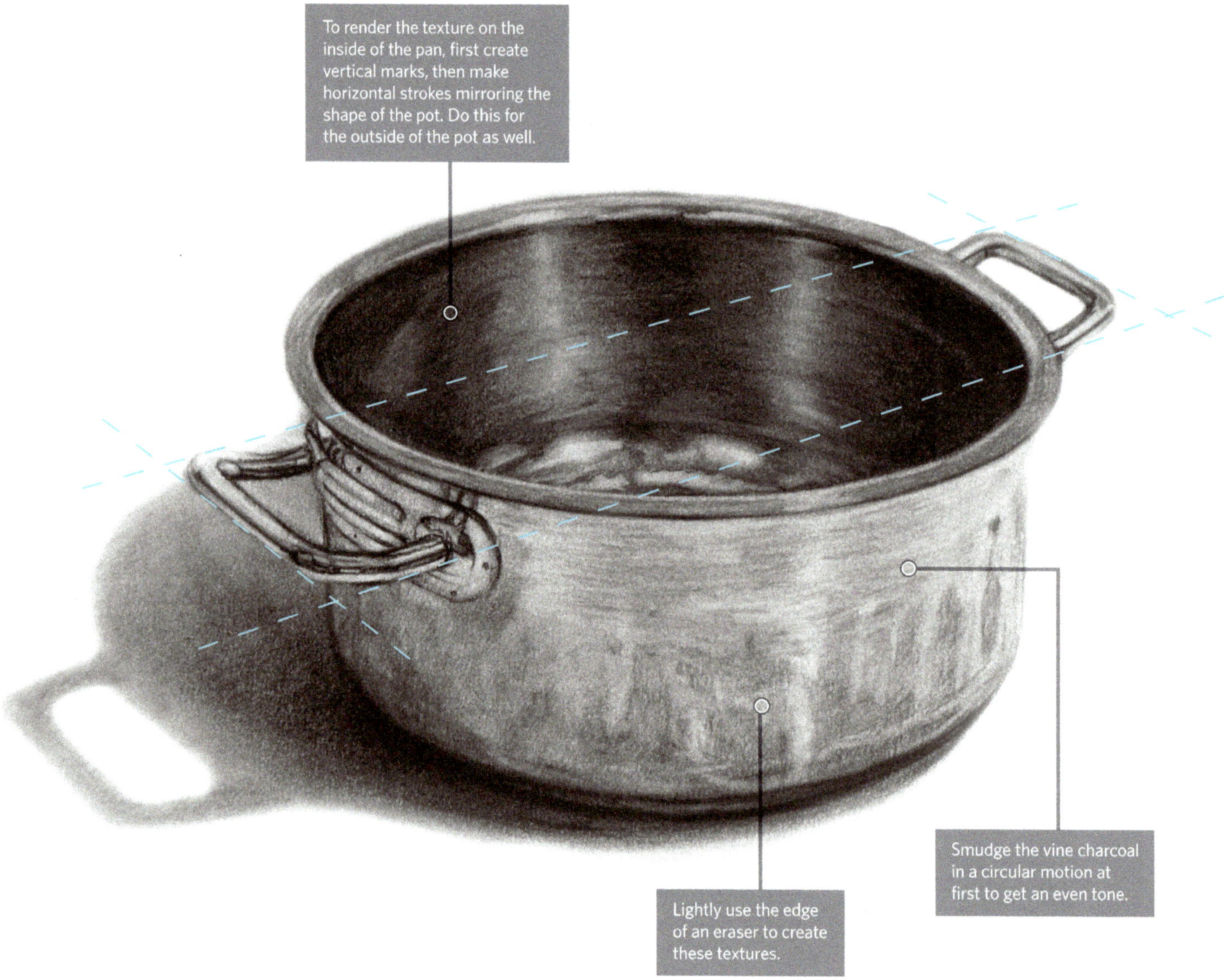

Now try drawing the pot yourself.

Drawing the pot will combine your skills from practicing with metal and from drawing the frying pan. Remember the inside of the pot will be darker than the outside, and pay attention to the bands of light on both the inside and outside. To properly capture the volume of the pot, make sure to render the sides using vertical motion, then go back into it using horizontal strokes that follow the shape of the pot. As always, work from general to specific.

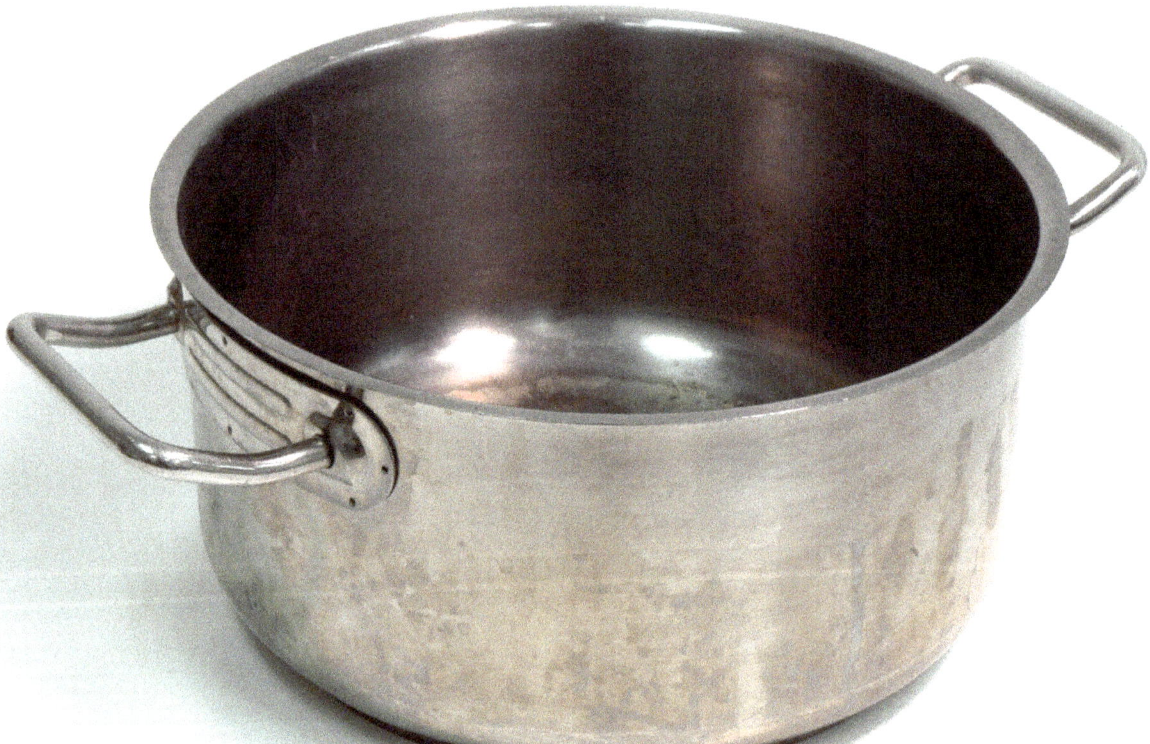

Now try drawing the pot using the reference picture without any grid lines.

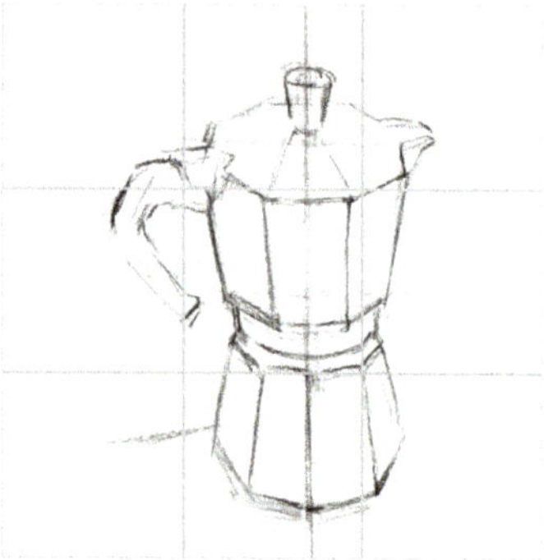

Sketch the general composition of the pot using vine charcoal.

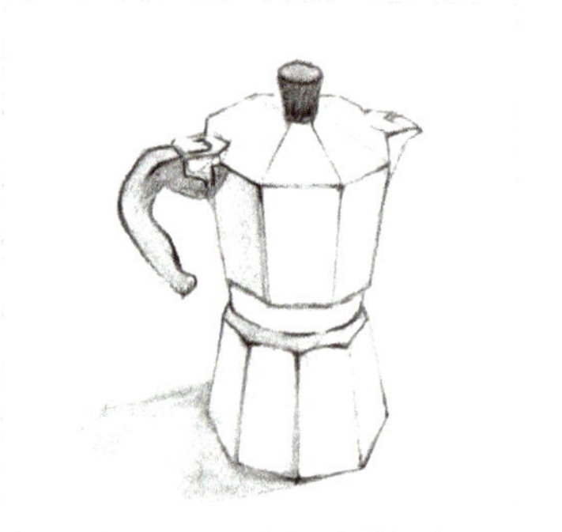

Identify the direction of the light source and shade in the general areas of shadow using vine charcoal.

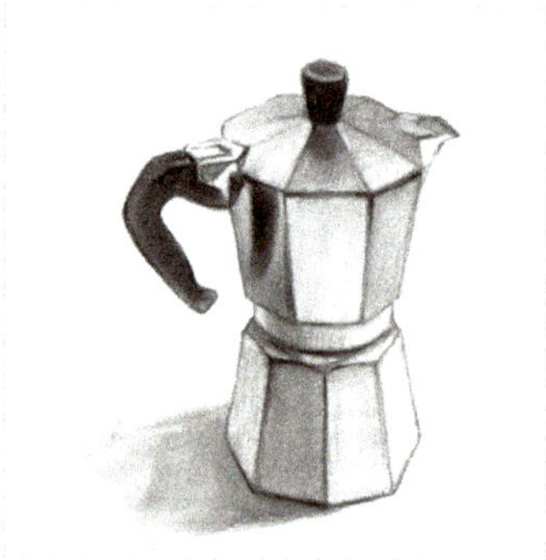

Continue to identify the darks, lights, and middle tones using a combination of vine and compressed charcoal.

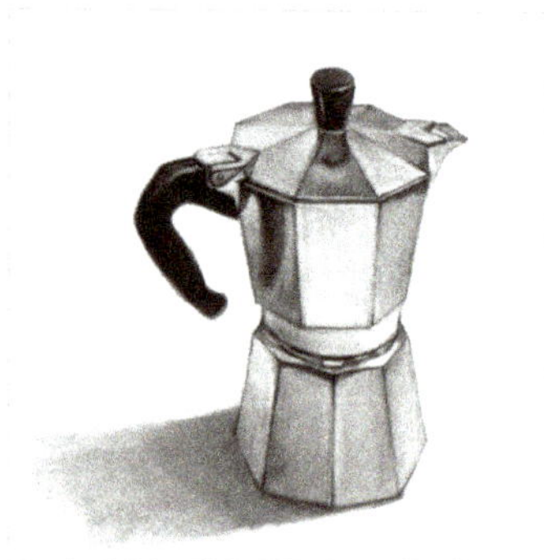

Make sure your espresso coffee pot drawing is fully defined, add different levels of darkness for each plane and create the highlights with an eraser.

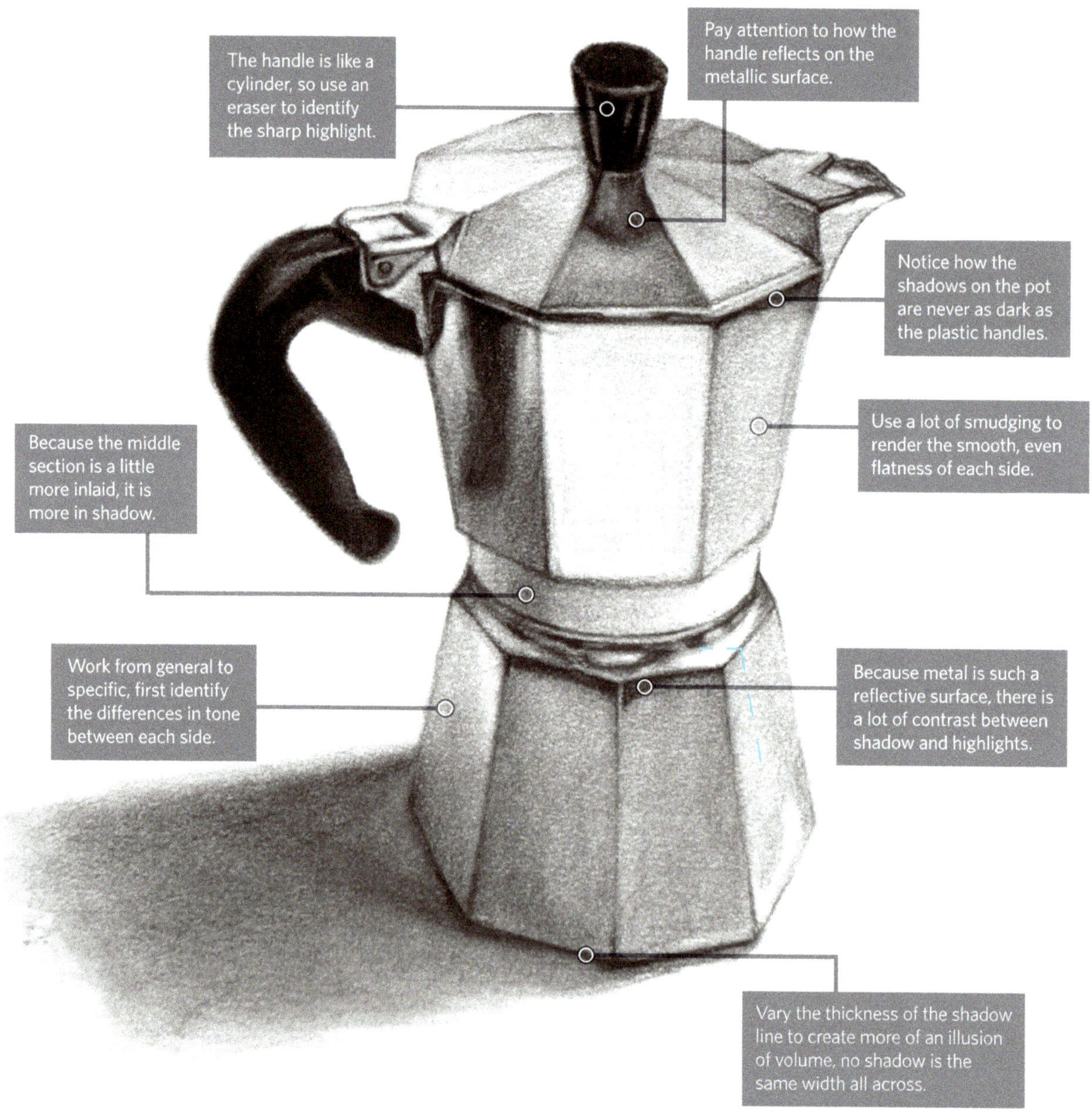

Now try drawing the expresso pot yourself.

For this exercise, focus on the way light reflects on the two different textures: black plastic and metal. Note that the metallic surface of the espresso pot is more reflective than the black plastic, which is why the handles are reflected onto the metallic surface of the espresso pot is more reflective than the black plastic, which is why the handles are reflected onto the metallic surface. Keep in mind that the espresso pot is shaped like a cylinder with eight sides so as to help you render its shape, like a cube but with more sides. Because the espresso pot has more sides, there are more tonal differences between each side.

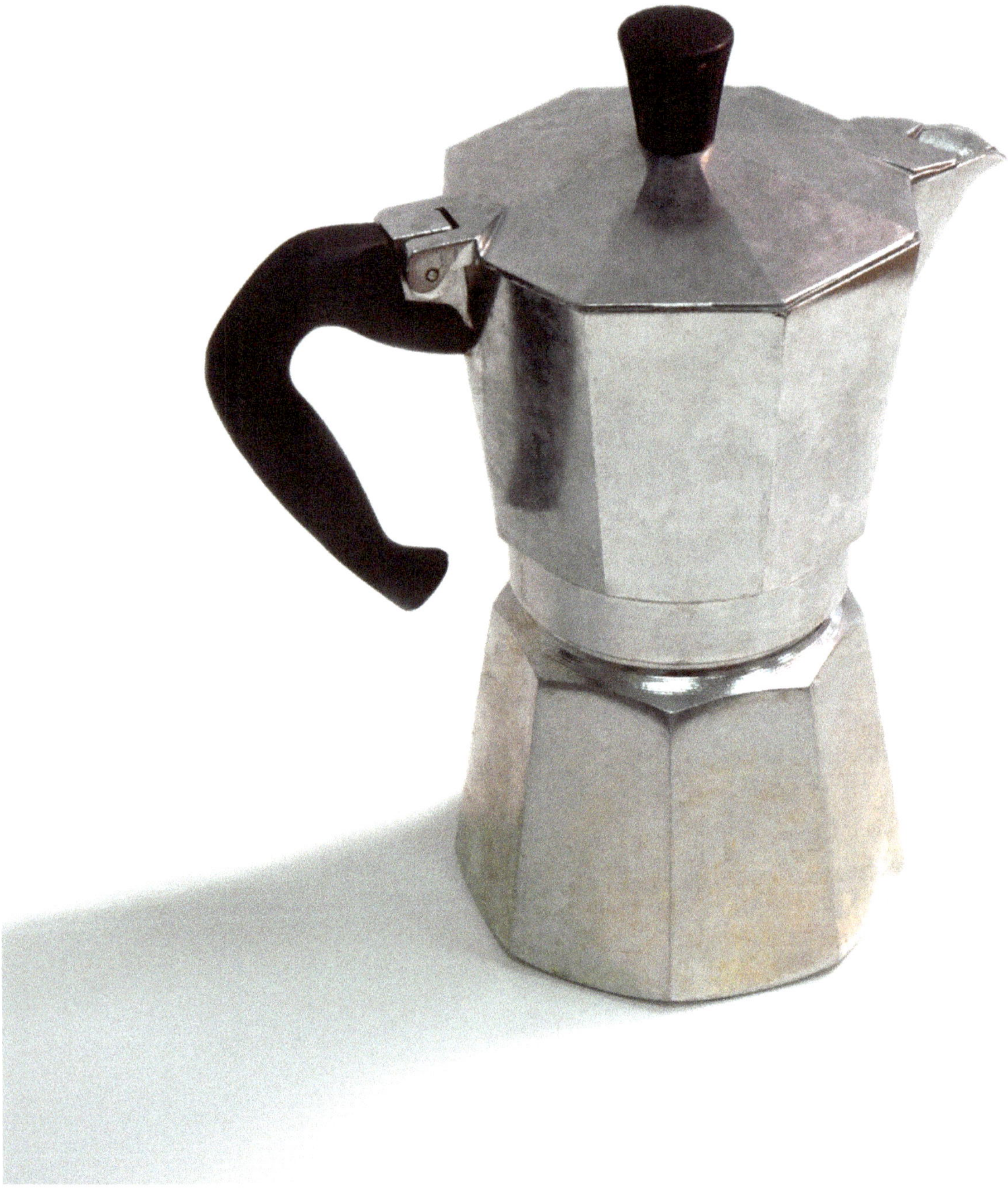

Now try drawing the espresso pot using the reference picture without any grid lines.

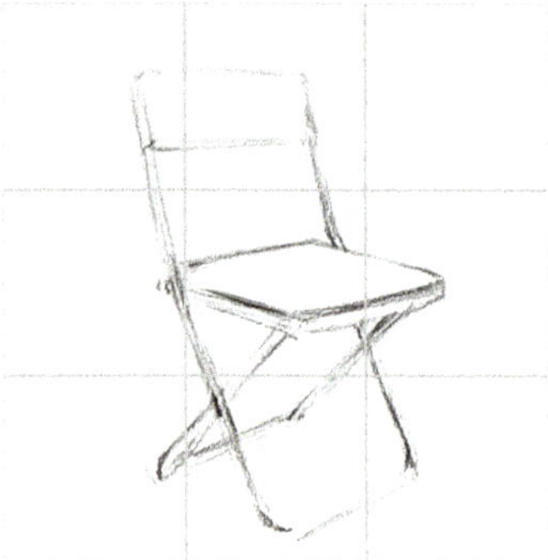

Sketch the general composition of the chair using vine charcoal.

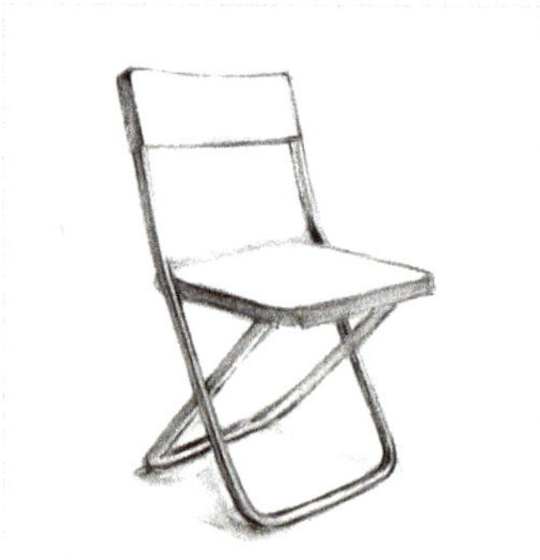

Identify the direction of the light source and shade in the general areas of shadow using vine charcoal.

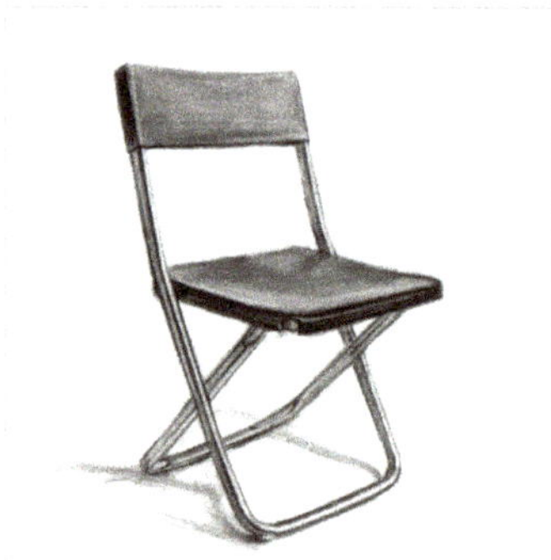

Continue to identify the darks, lights, and middle tones using a combination of vine and compressed charcoal.

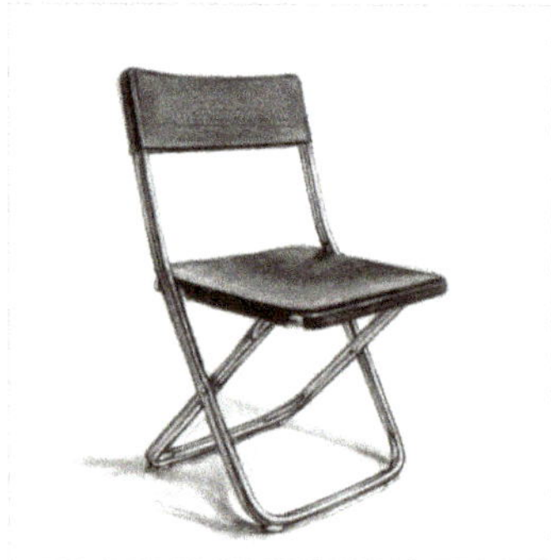

Make sure your folding chair drawing is fully defined; pay attention to the contrast in dark and light.

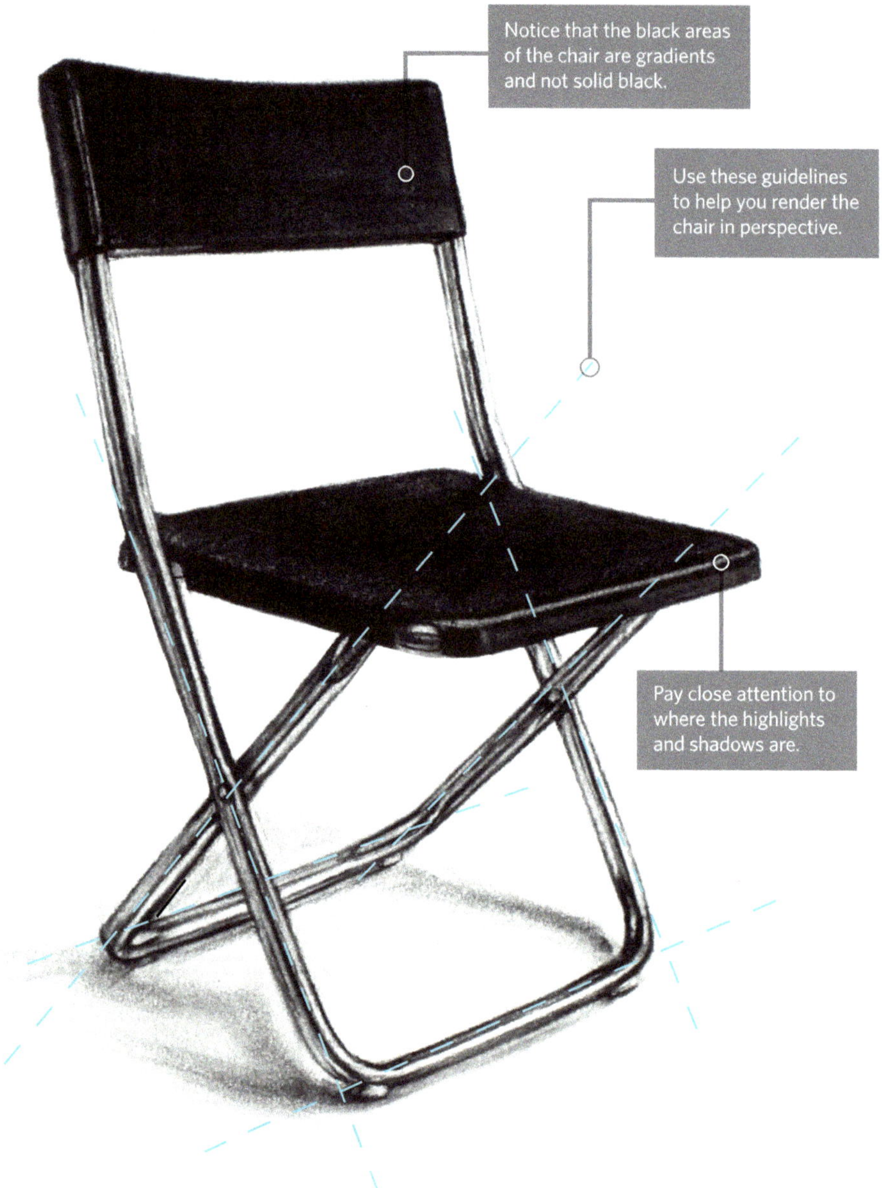

Now try drawing the chair yourself.

The chair may seem like an easy exercise, but there are many small nuiances and subtles details. Perspective is very important in rendering a realistic chair, therefore, make sure to sketch out perspective lines to guide you in rendering the chair. After rendering the general tones, pay close attention to the edges where the black plastic bends and to the contrasting highlights and shadows of the metallic areas.

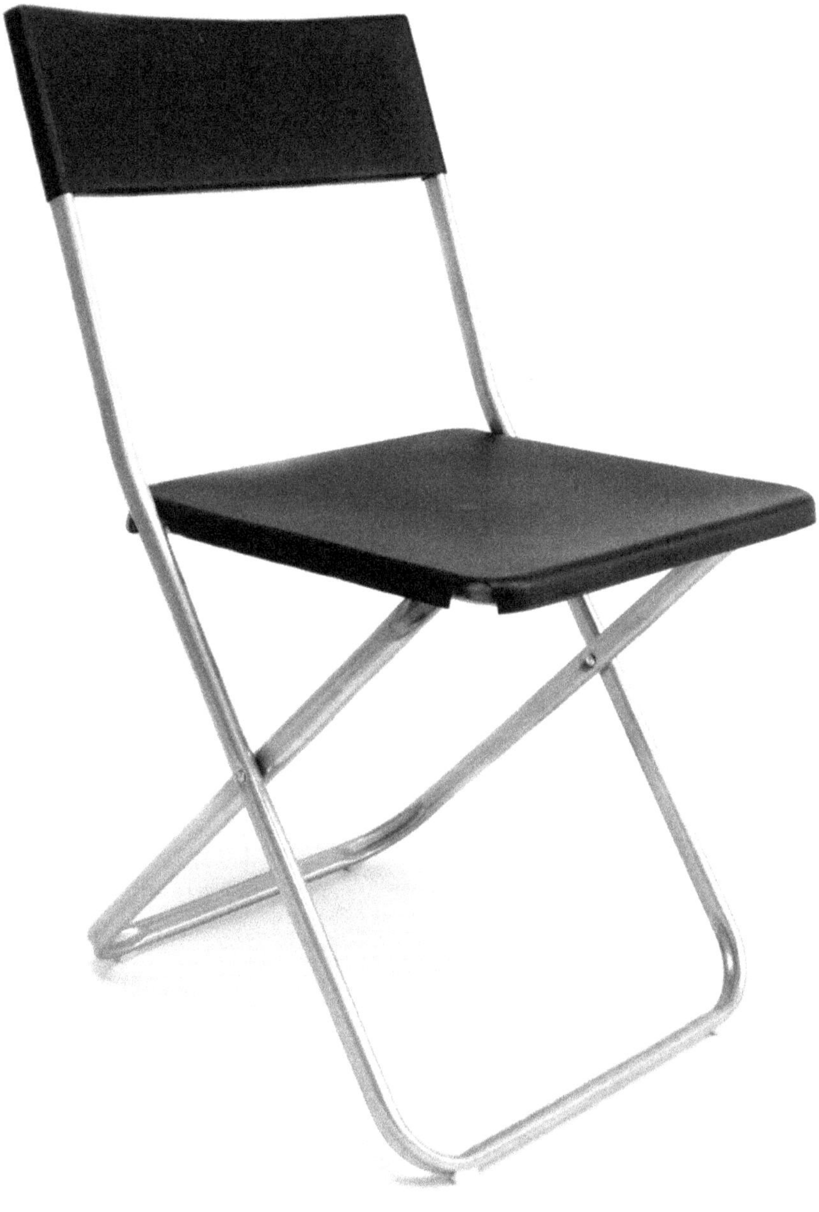

Now try drawing the chair using the reference picture without any grid lines.

ABOUT OOGIE HAUS

Oogie Haus is an art foundation unique for its diverse artistic endeavors, including an emphasis in art education, art & design internship opportunities, and volunteer outreach programs. There have been several book publications as well, such as "Art College Admissions," an insightful guideline for students applying to art schools.

Besides being an educational resource, Oogie Haus functions dually as an art gallery and art dealership. Through its research, it seeks to contribute a bigger network for local and international artists simultaneously curating its unique voice in todays art world. For more information please visit www.oogiehaus.com

ABOUT THE AUTHOR

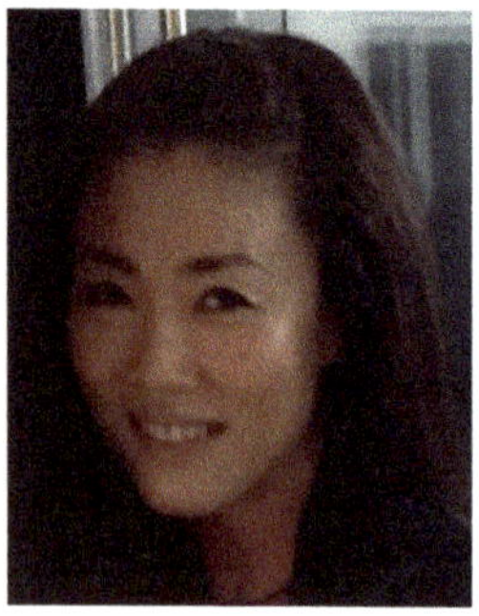

WOOK CHOI is an accomplished art dealer, education columnist, author, art educator, art gallerist, and art portfolio consultant who has guided over a thousand students to college admissions and scholarship success during the course of her 31-year teaching career.
She has received widespread recognition for her teaching methods from Mayor Michael Bloomberg; former First Lady Laura Bush; the New York Commissioner of Education, Richard P. Mills; US Congress member, Jerrold Nadler; the Alliance for Young Artists; YoungArts; and the Marie Walsh Sharpe Foundation. For more information, please visit www.wookchoi.com.

CHECK OUT SOME OF OUR OTHER BOOKS

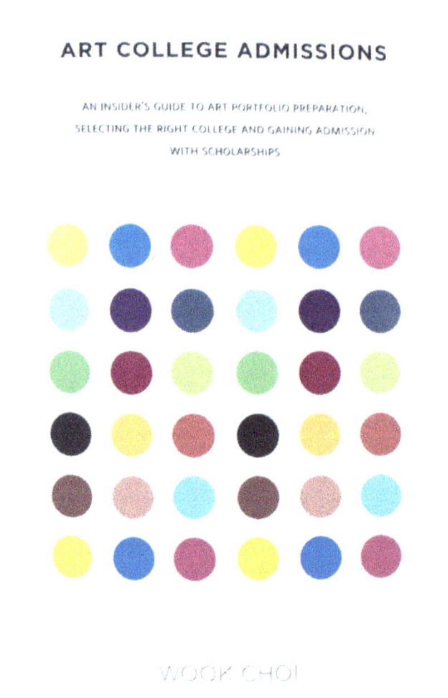

ART COLLEGE ADMISSIONS

An insider's guide to portfolio preparation, selecting the right college and gaining admission with scholarships.
In the first half of this book, you'll learn how vital a role art plays in the success of businesses today, what admissions committees at top art colleges really look for when deciding who to admit, and essential tips for developing award-winning art portfolio pieces. In the second half, you'll learn about the distinct advantages and histories of the most highly-ranked and popular art colleges in the Northeast, specific and actionable tips for getting into each school, and any changes these schools have made to their admissions criteria in recent years.

YOU CAN CONTINUE TO DEVELOP YOUR ARTISTIC SKILLS IN DIFFERENT MEDIA!

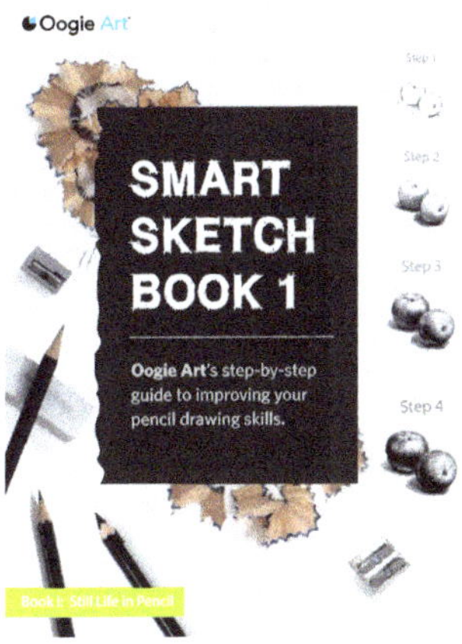

SMART SKETCHBOOK 1:
Still Life in Pencil

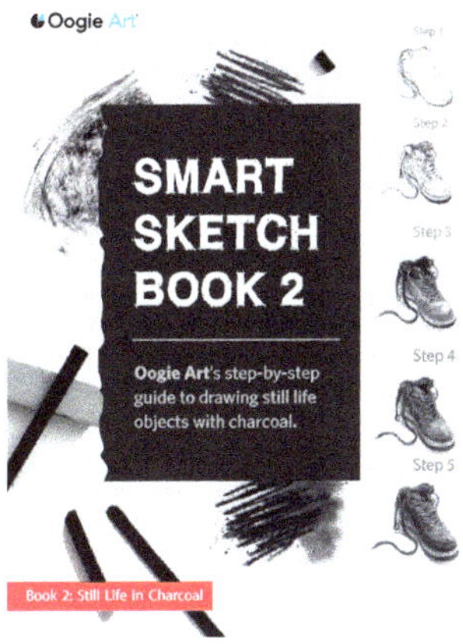

SMART SKETCHBOOK 2:
Still Life in Charcoal

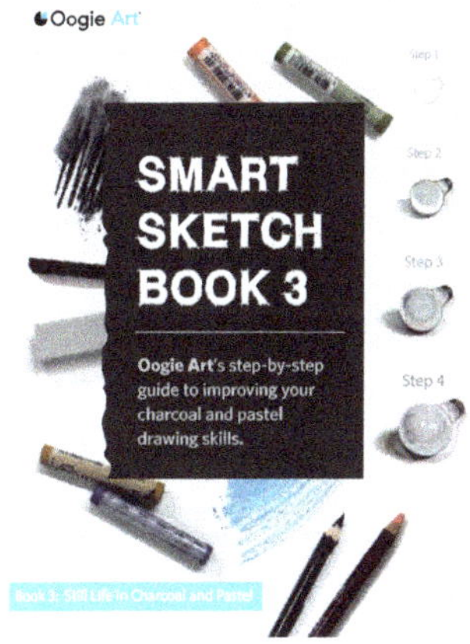

SMART SKETCHBOOK 3:
Still Life in Charcoal and Pastel

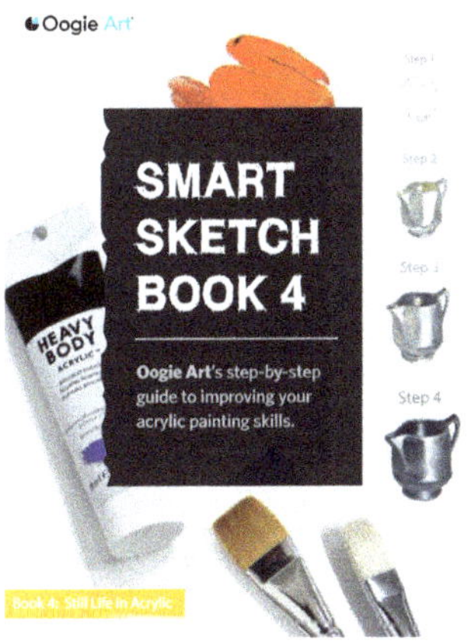

SMART SKETCHBOOK 4:
Still Life in Acrylic

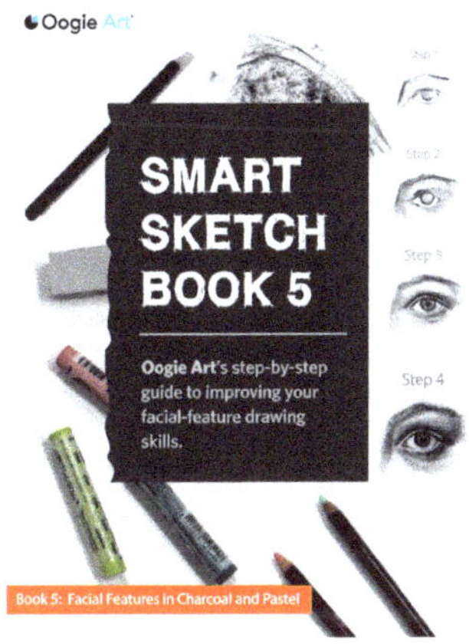

SMART SKETCHBOOK 5:
Facial Features in Charcoal and Pastel

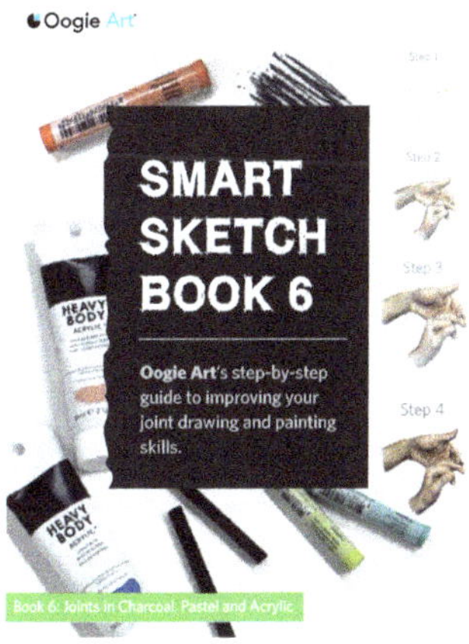

SMART SKETCHBOOK 6:
Joints in Charcoal, Pastel and Acrylic

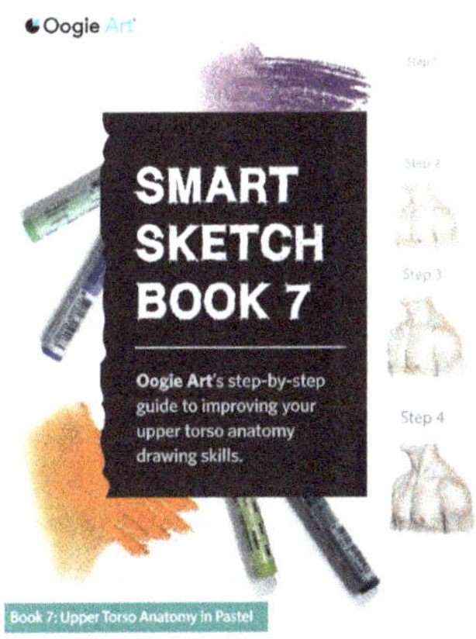

SMART SKETCHBOOK 7:
Upper Torso Anatomy in Pastel

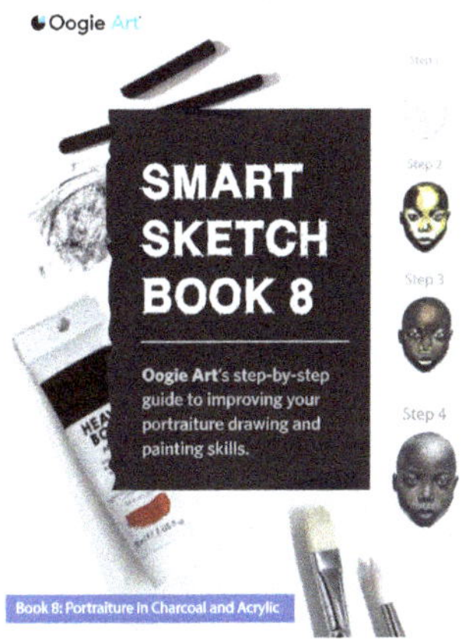

SMART SKETCHBOOK 8:
Portraiture in Charcoal and Acrylic

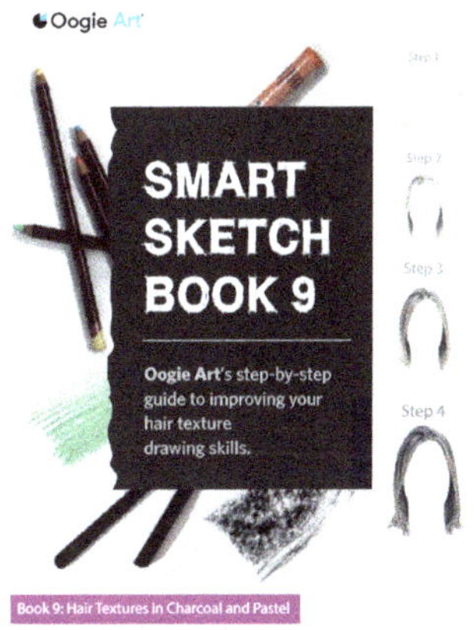

SMART SKETCHBOOK 9:
Hair Textures in Charcoal and Pastel

www.ingramcontent.com/pod-product-compliance
Ingram Content Group UK Ltd.
Pitfield, Milton Keynes, MK11 3LW, UK
UKHW062010290726
14090UKWH00022B/1482